Working the Double Shift

Working the Double Shift

A Young Woman's Journey with Autism

Christine Motokane
Edited by Hope Glennon

Rev. date: 02/12/2014

To order additional copies of this book, contact:
Xlibris LLC
1-888-795-4274
www.Xlibris.com
Orders@Xlibris.com
542587

Contents

Chapter 1

Introduction

My name is Christine and I'm a 21-year old female living with autism. This is probably one of the few books about autism that is written by one of my gender or an individual living with autism for that matter. A lot of the books out there are written in the second person by professionals and parents of the autism community. That being the case, I couldn't find one single autism book that I could relate to. These books are not written in the first person. Instead, the writers are usually conveying the perspective of their children and or clients. Therefore the inaccuracies are many.

My book is going to be different. It's not going to sound clinical or like an instruction manual. It's going to be about my life, perspective, accomplishments and the challenges that I've faced and overcome. The intention of this book is to give hope for families, especially to parents of young children. For professionals who work with those diagnosed with autism. I also intend to reach all the autistic individuals out there as well as anyone else interested in becoming first hand educated in this field.

To give you a brief introduction about myself, I was diagnosed with autism at age four by a local regional center. It was with the help of intensive therapy that I was able to develop normal language and verbal skills. For the last 16 years, and probably for the rest of my life, autism will always be with me. However, over the years I have learned to accept it. Living with the disorder has taught me to always be myself in a neurotypical society and to not care so much about what other people think of me. It was this thinking that I decided to spread tolerance and acceptance, and to give advice to families that inspired me to write this book. I want to make a difference in this world and to educate society enough to understand that people living with autism have thoughts and feelings just like any other human on this planet.

The first few chapters of my book are a recollection of my early years. Like the variety of other books written on this topic, it is according to my parents. But when I get up to sharing the history of my middle school, high school and college years, it becomes more of my perspective and voice since I can remember those experiences very well. When reading this book, you will see how I learned how to become a self advocate and as I've previously mentioned, the challenges I've faced associated with this very often misunderstood syndrome.

Chapter 2

Infancy and Early Childhood

After five years of marriage my parents developed their professional careers like many married couples and decided thereafter to start a family. Although, my grandfather who was an avid golfer would say: "I'm not sure which will come first; my first grandchild or first 'hole-in-one!" by mid-1991 he had yet to get his first "hole-in-one" but was elated when he learned my mother was pregnant with me and he was going to be a grandfather. The due date was in April of the year 1992.

Over the next nine months my parents prepared for the big day. My mother was very diligent about following all the prenatal advice from the likes of "What to Expect When You're Expecting" and her OB/GYN. The only thing my parents knew about me going into the final trimester was I had two legs, two arms and was probably a female based on the doctor's interpretation of the ultra-sound. My father said he felt relieved that he was going to have a daughter because he wasn't sure he could keep up with a son who wanted to play sports or go camping.

As for my mother, she went into labor two weeks before her due date. Her water broke the day after she started her maternity leave and she wasn't experiencing any contractions. Following the doctor's orders they raced over to the hospital just to be checked out.

The doctor shared with my parents that there wasn't a lot of amniotic fluid so they decided to induce labor with a hefty dose of pitocin. After 36 hours of labor I was finally born on March 23rd at 4:00 p.m. There I was a 6 pound 10 ounce healthy girl and first grandchild for both sets of grandparents. One of my aunts had fraternal twins (a boy and a girl) eight months after I was born. So my grandfather never got his "hole-in-one" but he was the proud recipient of three glowing grandchildren.

My parents said I was a great baby because I slept a lot. From the moment I exited my mother's womb and for the following four weeks I slept more than I was awake. I was a lazy eater and gave my mother great frustration during breast feeding. In fact, my lack of latching on resulted in my mother's first and only episode of post partum blues.

For the first six months I was your ordinary loveable baby and gave tremendous joy to my parents and both grandparents. I always wanted to be held by one of my parents. If either of my parents tried to put me down on a blanket or in a crib I would cry until they came and picked me up again. The only thing that would allow my parents to be hands free of me was a mechanical swing that would calm me down.

Christmas 1992 was a special one for my parents. It was my first and they wanted to make sure it was one that we all remembered. I had gifts from my parents, grandparents and all my aunts and uncles, so when Christmas morning came my parents were all prepared with their camera. When the first present was put in front of me I'm sure my parents expected me to smile and rip the wrapping paper off to see my present. My dad was a little surprised how passively I looked at the gift and that I was more mesmerized by the wrapping paper than the present itself. It seemed odd but my parents thought nothing of it.

Throughout my infant and toddler years, I didn't have as much speech compared to other children my age. When I did speak, it was mostly fragmented and also engaged in a little bit of echolalia. I repeated words what was said to me. I didn't respond to my name nor engage in pretend play which was typical of most toddlers. I had a bizarre attachment to strange objects. An example of such behavior was when I was in daycare I would not interact with the other children but would instead play with the tail of a rocking horse. On top of the speech and social issues, my parents were having trouble toilet training me. I was so used to going in my diaper that it was hard to go on the toilet. It wasn't until at the age of four that I was fully trained.

Noticing all of my delays and odd behaviors, my parents took me in to get diagnosed. Unfortunately, I didn't get my diagnosis right away because everyone thought I had ADHD because of my hyperactivity. However, I wasn't a severe enough case meaning that I didn't have any self injurious behaviors such as head banging nor any sleep problems. It wasn't until December of 1996 where I was referred to the regional center that I got my official diagnosis. At first the people at the center weren't sure if it was autism or PDD. But, when the clinical psychologist came to evaluate me I was having a bad day and as a result I was showing a lot of the traits associated with autism like self stimulation. Getting an autism diagnosis wasn't easy for my parents especially my dad. Hoping for a less severe diagnosis than autism, my dad asked the doctor if she was sure if I had Aspergers Syndrome. The doctor told my parents that I definitely had autism and the symptoms that I had matched that of autistic disorder even though I was considered to be a mild case. My mom took it well but my dad had a little bit of a tougher time. Recently my dad told me that he called a previous therapist who evaluated me. My dad said "I can deal with ADHD but I don't know if I can deal with autism". This was due to the fact that he didn't have a lot of knowledge about positive outcomes for individuals on the autistic spectrum.

Luckily for me, my parents didn't give up on me. My mother actually left her job to be a stay at home mom so she could take care of me and help me achieve the best life possible. They weren't like other parents who sat in a puddle of denial. They were proactive and took me to many therapists. The therapies ranged from speech therapy, to occupational therapy to social skills group etc. My mother would drive sometimes long distances to take me to these therapies. If it weren't for that I wouldn't be the talkative person I am today.

When I started preschool, I was placed in a special class with other children that had various disabilities. This was the case because the school district didn't think a regular preschool class with typically developing children was appropriate for me at the time. Being in that classroom brought on some new challenges. The teacher in charge of that classroom had no clue on how to deal with children like me. She had an emergency teaching credential and was not qualified to teach a class that had students with special needs. I had serious sensory issues which prevented me from sitting still and I was full of hyperactivity. Because of all my delays and the fact I couldn't sit still, the teacher thought I should be held back another year in preschool. My mother thought that I wasn't making much progress in the preschool classroom and sent me to a six week program at UCLA.

During my time there I was given an intelligence test in which I scored poorly on and the person who administered the test thought I had mental retardation. The lady who administered the test was a young graduate student who was new to the field. My mother didn't agree with the test results. So she talked to the program director, who then told my mom that I was given the wrong test. I made a lot of progress at UCLA. The preschool teacher observed me at the program and she thought she was seeing a different child. After I was discharged from the program, I resumed in the preschool class and was able to proceed onto kindergarten. The doctor who ran the program at UCLA told my mom that I was going to be high functioning and that academics wouldn't be a problem. However, I would struggle socially. I believe that statement is a true depiction of me today since I do well in school but have a hard time making friends. It was at UCLA where we started using the term "high-functioning autism".

Chapter 3

Elementary School
Kindergarten-4th Grade

In kindergarten, I was placed in a pilot program for kids with autism. Eventually I was able to join a general education classroom for the second half of the school year. Sometimes though I would go back to the special education classroom I had been in because I felt more comfortable there. Kindergarten was the year I noticed that I loved jumping up and down. There was a jungle gym that I loved to climb in the play yard and rather than playing with the other children I would be on top of that thing and watch the other children play with each other. One day I thought it was a good idea to bring my toy bugs to school and put them on the jungle gym. Unfortunately for me one of the teaching assistants took them away. This caused me to become very distressed because those toy bugs brought me comfort and solace. Having them taken away was devastating, like I lost something precious. I cried hard. The reason I am sharing this story because I want to demonstrate that when I was little, I didn't have any connection to people and felt more of a connection to my toys.

Although my speech improved by kindergarten, my fine motor skills were poor. I couldn't even pick up a pencil and do basic handwriting. When my mom saw another boy with autism able to pick up a pencil and write his own name, she began to worry. It became questionable whether or not I would function in a regular classroom. As a result my mom worked intensively on my handwriting. She bought stencils with all the letters of the alphabet for me to trace. I also used a pencil grip to help me hold the pencil in the right manner. In a short period of time, I was able to master the skill of writing just in time for first grade.

At the end of my kindergarten year, it was decided that I could be fully included in the general education classroom with my typically developing peers with a part-time aide. My elementary years were pleasant and ideal for a child with autism or other disabilities. I was never bullied, pitied or excluded. The kids at my school were very accepting. In fact I made friends easily during those years. I would have play dates with some of my classmates and was invited to their birthday parties. Since I was treated so well at my school, I forgot I even had a disability. However, I still went to all my therapies once a week until the second grade. I also attended tutoring on weekdays after school and a social skills group on the weekends. This was taught by a young and energetic educational therapist whom I met while I attending the early intervention program at UCLA. Along with some therapies, I also tried out some extracurricular activities such as the Special Olympics for two years and piano lessons for two years. However I stopped all these activities in my fifth grade year because the school work got too intense.

One of the best teachers that I had in school was my third grade teacher. She was an outgoing Asian American woman who accepted me and treated me like all the other children. She was engaging with the class and came up with creative lessons and projects. I did projects such as telling a joke to the class, coming up with a creative invention and a teaching the class project. My teacher would also tell personal stories of her son and her dog which made us all laugh. We also went on field trips to different places. My favorite field trip is when we went to The Manhattan Beach Roundhouse Aquarium. At the end of the year, we had a zoologist come in and he showed us different types of animals from tiny foxes to reptiles. Each of my classmates got a video that highlighted some of the activities we did during the year so we could always remember 2000 to 2001. Third grade was a great year because I was exposed to different experiences. I felt that I grew academically from them. Every few years my third grade class would have a reunion where we would meet up and reminisce about the good old days.

In my late elementary school years, I went through a phase where I didn't like wearing long pants or jeans. Looking back, I think this can be attributed to the sensory issues where I didn't like things touching my ankles. I would only wear shorts and capri pants to school. This caused a huge burden for my mom when shopping for clothes for me since capri pants were hard to find and she was worried that on cooler days I would freeze to death with part of my legs left exposed. I never did feel cold and it wasn't until the sixth grade that I started wearing pants again.

Even though my classmates accepted me and I had friends during my elementary school years, autism still got in the way in my daily life. For one thing, I needed to "stim"(self stimulation) with pens and rubber bands.

In case you don't know what "stimming" is it is an activity which provides a "calming sensation" to the person with autism. For me, I would stare at pens and rubber bands and twirled them in front of my eyes. My parents would ask me what I would see when I looked at them. I told them I saw colors and another world that reflected my own. It was my way of processing the world around me. I also preferred to be alone especially during recess and lunch. During this time I would just jump up and down around the play yard all by myself. My urge to jump was something I constantly needed to do. It began to consume my time. I needed to do it at home and at school. I will discuss in a later chapter that this urge was related to the sensory issues that I had.

Towards the middle of fourth grade, I was fully aware that I was entering puberty. Until then I thought that I wouldn't develop these "grown-up traits" until I was my mother's age. Beginning puberty was hard because I was still a young nine-year-old girl but my body had plans of its own. The hardest part for both my mom and I was that there weren't too many books out there that dealt with puberty. The thing that helped explain this radical change was a book called *American Girl*. Another factor that made entering puberty hard was that I started far earlier than other girls my age which made me feel very awkward and insecure about my body. As a result, I didn't want to wear bras because I felt they were too grown up for me and I was the only one wearing one. I tried to wear loose t-shirts so that my 'breast buds' wouldn't show through my shirts. My mom had an ongoing battle in trying to get me to see the importance of wearing one. She explained that prevailing norm was that women wore bras to hold their breasts into place as well as preserving their modesty. However, I didn't know what was considered standard practices because I was far so preoccupied with just being a kid.

Chapter 4

Fifth Grade: the year of changes

Fifth grade was the year that things really started to change for me. It was the year of many firsts and when I started to show some awareness that I was different. Even though it was over ten years ago, I remembered key details and events that happened vividly that year. It was a paradoxical year full of laughter and anxiety. I'll go into further detail later on in my story.

On my first day of school, I experienced a major change that signaled I was growing up. It wasn't subtle. To put it simply, I started my first period. Unfortunately it came at a time when I wasn't ready for it. Even though I had a body of a young woman I still had a mind of a child. Just like how I reacted when I first noticed my developing breasts, I felt awkward and insecure. To try to maintain my childhood, I would pretend as if I had never menstruated. My aide and my mom at school had to help me manage my menstrual cycle. The start of my period was the first of the many changes to come.

Even though I had an awkward start of the school year, it actually was a great year for me. I started to get out of my autistic shell and started socializing more with my classmates. Before, I would be in my own little world and although I knew the names of my classmates, I didn't have full blown conversations with them. I started to use humor to reach out to people. It all started with a TV show on *Nickelodeon* hosted by a teen actress. The show would feature different characters acting out skits which were pretty funny. I noticed that the people were laughing whenever the characters did something comedic. Seeing the attention that these characters on the show got from being silly made me want to do some of the same things with my peers and teacher so that they would like me. Luckily for me, my plan worked. My peers thought my jokes were funny and as a result they all wanted to hang out with me. They would approach me and asked me to tell more jokes. The most popular jokes that I would tell were "knock-knock" jokes. Today I would think this type of humor is corny. But, it was elementary school after all, and in the end they helped me achieve my goal. It also gave me a sense of empowerment and raised my self esteem because I felt that people were finally realizing that I have a lot of unique qualities and gifts. They say that people with autism don't have a sense of humor but hopefully this story will convey to people that this stereotype is far from true.

Despite some of the triumphs I made socially that year, there were some tough times as well. It was the year I was getting ready to transition to middle school. I didn't know that after this year I would have to go to a new school until I saw a book that my mom picked up and it was titled "Getting Ready for Middle School". That wasn't subtle. Reading that title made me very anxious. I didn't want to go to a new school. I had been attending my elementary school for six years. On top of everything else, my parents felt that the school district in which I was currently attending was not going to give me the help I needed in order to make my middle school years a success. My parents decided to search different neighborhoods where it was covered by different school districts. They finally settled in a beach community in the South Bay area of Los Angeles. I didn't want to move out of my old house. Another huge change I wasn't ready for. The combination of transitioning to a new school and new neighborhood caused me such anxiety that I would just cry. The transition from elementary school to middle school made me discover that anxiety brings out the worst of my autism.

Yet another change that happened that year was that the aide who had been with me since the first grade decided to leave midyear which left me three more months of school in which I needed assistance. This aide was a bubbly African American woman named Yolanda who formed a bond with all of my classmates. My peers didn't see her as an aide who was helping me get through the day but as an adult they could go to for help. Even though Yolanda was with me part time, she would accompany me on class field trips. We had our moments during our time together. She would have to redirect me to stay on task and to make sure I was organized with my desk. To try to motivate me to organize my desk, Yolanda came up with the idea of a "neat fairy" that was going to check to make sure my desk was in shape. I didn't like the system she came up with and I actually removed the labels she put on my desk to help keep me in line. But she tolerated all of my rebellion. She was one of many aides who really understood me even though she had no formal education that made her 'qualified.' Yolanda's departure was very hard on me since we had grown very close.

Fortunately, my fifth grade teacher Ms. B was awesome. She was a young woman in her 20's and had been teaching at my school for one year. Even though Ms. B was a general education teacher, I felt she understood me more than some of the special education teachers I had during my school years. Ms. B appreciated my goofy sense of humor and even encouraged it. She would also open her class up and allow students to eat in at lunch time. In fact, when I didn't like what they served in the cafeteria, Ms. B would offer some of her lunch to me. Ms. B and Yolanda were the first of many people who came into my life who didn't have special ed "credentials" who were there for me and understood my autism.

Fifth grade was also the year I learned about my autism diagnosis. I don't remember exactly how I found out but my dad recently told me that he remembered having a conversation with me about my diagnosis and explained how my brain was "wired" differently from other people. I had already noticed that there was something different about me. I noticed my peers were developing more mature interests and were growing out of dolls and pretend play while I was still hanging with Barbie. In fact when I would go over to one of my friend's house, all I would want to do is play with dolls while she was interested in other things like boys. Signs of my autism were becoming more apparent. I was kind of forced to learn about my diagnosis but it wasn't easy. When I learned what autism was, I felt sick because there was something wrong with me. It didn't help that my mom was part of an organization that wanted to cure autism. Even the name of the organization had the word "cure" in it which pierced my self esteem. Learning about what this organization stood for gave me my first exposure to what the public's perception of autism actually was. Their focus was to make the autistic population more "normal", as though we had to be fixed. This was the beginning and for years after I made it my mission to change this superficial perspective. Over time I began to accept my diagnosis as a part of who I am. I mean 'normal' means usual right? Well, I happen to be quite unusual. I am unique. That being said 'full' acceptance of my autism was no easy task. Looking back however, I was glad that I learned about my diagnosis at age 10 because it saved me from the confusion and depression that people who get diagnosed later often face.

At the end of fifth grade, I received a presidential academic award that was signed by President George W. Bush. I felt honored because only two people in my class got this award and I was one of them. It also showed that people with autism are capable students. Getting recognized by the president for strong academic achievement has begun to destroy those myths and show what people with autism and Aspergers are really made of. However, there are still professionals and parents out there that question our capacity and therefore relegate us to special education classrooms. Clearly my work here is not yet done.

Chapter 5

New School-New Neighborhood

The summer of 2003 was a hard one. I had to deal with transitioning to middle school and living in a new neighborhood. My mom enrolled me at a middle school preparation class during the summer. It was the only year I didn't go to a summer camp since we were new to the area and the summer camps I went to in my old neighborhood were too far of a drive. Instead I went to a teen center that was run by the city's recreational services. I thought that joining the teen center was a way to meet the other kids who will be attending middle school with me. Plus, my friend that I knew since I was two years old would be going to the teen center too. Unfortunately, the majority of kids in the program did not live in the area and I was bullied. I've never been bullied in elementary school nor was I bullied in future years after this incident. There was a mean boy who would call me names. The bullying started when I was playing air hockey against this boy and he started calling me a "loser" for no apparent reason. He also called me "gay" when I was touching a punching bag that looked like a man. I didn't think to tell anyone about the situation since I didn't want to get the boy in trouble. But also because I was so naïve, I didn't know that I was being bullied. It wasn't until my friend told my mom what was going on that my mom decided to remove me from that program. She thought it was an unsupervised environment.

In August 2003, I got my first four-legged pet. In the past, all my pets were fish that only survived for one day to a few months. There was a stray rabbit that would go into my grandparents' backyard, and the amazing part about it was that the rabbit kept coming back. My grandfather got the idea of catching the rabbit one day and put it in a makeshift cage. I remember him calling us asking if we would want to have a pet rabbit. My mom was a little hesitant because she knew nothing about taking care of rabbits but we decided to give it a go. Well, to our surprise the bunny was surprisingly mellow and sweet. Along with her mellow personality, my rabbit was also potty trained which didn't give us the extra responsibility of cleaning up after her. We decided to name the bunny "Chocolate" because of her dark brown fur. Chocolate had a bond with my mom because she kept coming up to her and licking her. However there is a mischievous side to Chocolate too. She would destroy all of my toys when I didn't pay attention to her, dig up our carpet and chew on wires. She finally learned her lesson of not chewing wires when she got electrocuted one time and it curled some of her whiskers.

Chocolate came into my life at a much needed time when so much was going on. She became my companion to help me with the stresses of middle school. Today, Chocolate continues to be alive and well and is still living in my bedroom. I think it's important for people on the autism spectrum to have pets in their life since animals are not as judgmental as people at times can be.

In September of that same year, I started my first year of middle school. I've been dreading the start of school since it caused me so much anxiety. I actually remembered crying the day before school started because I was so nervous about whom my teachers would be and who would support me through the day. The first day didn't turn out so bad. I had math, my elective class, humanities block (at my school it is broken into three periods of history, reading and writing), adaptive physical education (I couldn't take regular physical education because of my poor hand eye coordination) and science. It was a long day since there were seven periods in a day with only lunch and nutrition for breaks.

My mom thought it would be a good idea to have an aide full-time for me because of the anxiety of being in this new environment. I also needed help with stress management. The aide who assisted me in sixth grade was really nice. Her name was Shelly. Both my mom and I liked her very much. Shelly was like a Yolanda for me at middle school. Shelly helped find some nice girls who I could sit with at lunch and during class. I always felt Shelly was on my side even when my case carrier at school wasn't which I will talk about later. My interaction with Shelly was not only at school but I saw her outside of school as well. She would "babysit" me when my parents wanted a night out for themselves. We would also hang out with her and her two children for lunch on the weekends. Her children were younger than me and would fight over which one of them got to play with me. Even though she broke some of the rules of professionalism by seeing me outside of school, my mom didn't seem to mind and was happy that Shelly wanted to spend time with me. Looking back, the reason Shelly related so well to me was that she herself was diagnosed with Asperger's Syndrome. I had no idea. With this new insight I remember realizing that once someone with Asperger's reaches adulthood their ability to hide their symptoms becomes significantly easier. This revelation helped quell some of the fears I had for my social future. Sixth grade turned out to be a relatively stable year. Everyone who went to my school knew each other from elementary school and I was considered the "new kid". I felt like I didn't belong in any group. I was one of the youngest students in my grade. Many of the students in my grade were a year older than me meaning they were all held back a year or they were placed an extra year in preschool. A lot of the girls were really precocious. There were girls who wore makeup to school and were into designer clothing which I didn't show an interest until later in high school. While I was wearing clothes from stores like Target, the other girls in my grade wore clothes from Abercrombie & Fitch and Juicy Couture. Seeing people in my grade dressing more mature made me feel insecure. It was now clear that there was a huge gap between myself and my typically developing peers. I still liked wearing kid's clothes and liked playing with dolls while the other sixth grade girls were already talking about boys and having crushes.

Sixth grade was the year that I learned the dynamics of teen friendships, groups and cliques. I watched movies and read books like *Mean Girls* to help me gain knowledge of the different social hierarchies and the different types of groups that I could identify. Unfortunately this knowledge worked against me because I don't do well in groups. There's always too much going on. As a result, I decided to stay under the radar and keep to myself since I didn't have the confidence to function any other way.

To help me get to know some of the students in my neighborhood, I enrolled in AYSO soccer throughout my middle school years. I've always liked playing soccer since I don't have to use my hands. My fine and gross motor skill issues prevent me from playing many sports like baseball, but playing soccer would give me some exercise. For two days out of the week I would have soccer practice. This actually made my schedule very intense since I had a lot of homework during sixth grade. But, it was worth it. Every weekend I had a soccer game. I was never excluded from playing soccer because of my special needs. The girls on my soccer team were really nice but I never saw them outside of soccer practice.

Luckily, I didn't fall behind in my assignments since my mom and my aide made sure I was getting homework done at home. However when it was time to plan my classes for seventh grade we decided that I would be put into resource English since the work load would be lighter than what I had in sixth grade.

My social life during this time was relatively stable. But I still missed my old friends. I lost contact with all of my friends from elementary school since I didn't live close to them anymore and I didn't feel comfortable using the phone to call them up. My social life then was great. So I had to adapt and get my social interactions from other students who also have a disability and my support people since I felt the most comfortable with them.

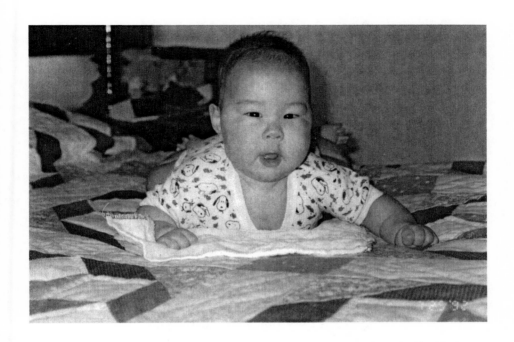

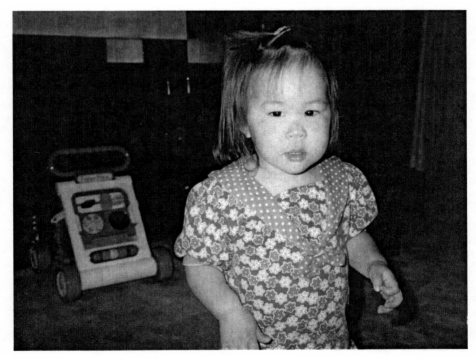

Chapter 6

The Seventh Grade Emotional Rollercoaster

My second year of middle school was probably my hardest year emotionally. While sixth grade was hard academically, seventh grade was one of those years that I just wanted to forget. It just was an emotional time for me because I was turning into a teenager. While being a twelve year-old preteen is hard for many girls it was especially hard for me as I couldn't control what would set me off.

The emotional frenzy started before the 2004-2005 school year began. The summer of 2004 was a year that was unforgettable as I had to watch the decline of my grandfather's (the one who caught the rabbit) health because he had liver cancer. I remember a week before his death; I witnessed my grandfather collapsing on to the ground while trying to go to the bathroom. It was a shocking experience for me since this was the first time I saw my grandfather helpless and I really thought he was going to die right in front of me. That was the last time I saw my grandfather alive. When my mom had to go care for him, I stayed home by myself because my dad was at work and was unable to watch me. This was the first time I stayed home alone. This was a huge step for me because I didn't think I was capable. But I was. In late August he officially lost his battle to liver cancer. I felt really devastated because he was the first grandparent that I ever lost. All four of my grandparents have been around my entire life. So this loss made me feel incomplete.

Shelly worked with me the beginning of seventh grade but it was only temporary. Health issues caused her to miss school a lot. In addition the school thought it was a good idea to put Shelly with another student who needed help going to a week long science camp. I was left with an inexperienced substitute aide and in certain classes I was left with no aide at all. This wouldn't have been a problem if I didn't have any behavioral issues that prevented me from sitting still in class. I remembered in science class, I was having one of those moments where I needed to be removed from class. However, there was no aide at the time to remove me. So there I was left weepy eyed and making a scene. Luckily some of my classmates tried to make me feel better but it also caused some unnecessary disruption. Had I had a trained aide with me that knew my escalation cycle that would have never happened. When my mom found out that I was left in one of my classes unattended, she became furious and even wrote an angry letter to the principal. She expressed how wrong it was of the school to put Shelly with another student without preparation or finding an experienced aide to take her place. It also disrupted my routine since I was used to Shelly being with me and having a new person working with me without preparation caused me to feel anxious which contributed to the reason for my outburst in science class.

As I mentioned in the previous chapter, I was placed in resource English so I can have a lighter homework load for seventh grade. However, the class didn't turn out as I expected. In fact it turned out to be a nightmare. Every time I was in the resource class I would have a meltdown and I would have to be escorted out of class.

In some instances I refused to come back into the room. On top of everything, some of the kids in that classroom were also disruptive. There was a boy in the class that kept bugging me. He would prevent me from concentrating in class by blurting out stupid stuff. There were other boys in that class who were also acting out and all of the sudden the class got out of control. Luckily the teacher and teaching assistant were nice but it was the rowdy behaviors of the boys that made being in resource English intolerable. None of the other students in my resource class had autism. But they did have various learning disabilities. It clearly wasn't a class for a student with autism who could do the work of a regular English class but couldn't deal with the stress of having so much homework. I remember one instance when I was having a bad day and I had to leave the classroom. While I was out one of the boys was physically removed from the class by a police officer for doing drugs. I later found this out because the therapist who I saw privately went to observe the class and saw the boy being dragged out. When it was time for my annual IEP meeting I was so done with resource classes that I actually told my parents and the staff who were present that I was "smarter" than most of my classmates. As harsh and politically incorrect as that sounded, the teacher actually agreed with me.

Another class that seemed to contribute to my outbursts was my math class. The teacher was new and although she was pleasant enough she had a hard time controlling her class. As a result some of the trouble making students would just dominate the class. Instead of teaching she would try to control the class by telling the disruptive students to be quiet. Because of these episodes I would go home not knowing how to do any of the homework. The teacher didn't have time to explain the concepts clearly. As a result I had to ask other people to help me.

The thing that really contributed to seventh grade being a chaotic year was getting a new aide who turned out to be the aide from hell. After Shelly left, I had three to four different aides working with me. Each one would cover an individual subject. I got along with all my aides except one, Gloria. This aide was clearly young and inexperienced compared to the other assistants who helped me throughout the day. She had an overly cold demeanor and never smiled at all. Whenever Gloria asked me to do something, she would talk to me in a disrespectful tone and would ask me to walk right next to her as if she didn't trust me. I felt Gloria saw me as a child with behavioral problems instead of someone who didn't have the tools to manage stress. I tried all I could to get a new aide but nobody listened to me because I was a student and therefore had no control. However, I was able to get another aide for one of my classes but I had to earn it by being good and respectful for Gloria in that class for one week which I managed to do. My mom made sure that the next school year Gloria wouldn't be working with me.

The inclusion teacher who acted like my case manager was not my favorite person to be around. Ms. Chu also had a distant demeanor which made her very unfriendly, closed minded and strictly professional. She didn't give me a hard time in my first year of middle school but she became more demanding in my second year. One time I tried to advocate for myself and Ms. Chu totally ignored what I had to say because she was the teacher and I was a student. She pulled rank. Not only that but I remember one time she lied to my mom. She told her that a class that I wanted to switch into wasn't offered when in fact it was. This was my first experience where a professional who was actually credentialed to work with special needs individuals didn't understand me. It was an eye opener and changed forever how I viewed those considered experts in their field. Just because someone holds a particular title doesn't mean they are equipped to deal with the likes of autism. (A perfect example here is Yolanda who without credentials to speak of on paper but changed my life to such a degree that I will be eternally grateful for having known her.) Having my feelings and voice disregarded by one of my members of my IEP team shattered my sense of self. It wasn't until many years later that I finally developed the confidence to believe that people would like to hear my voice and what it actually had to say.

Chapter 7

Eighth Grade: Another Interesting Year

Eighth grade was a very interesting year. It was not as bad as seventh grade but it still had its ups and downs. At the start of the 2005-2006 school year my mother decided to have a nonpublic agency work with me. My mom wanted someone that would help me improve my social skills and my stress management because of how hard my seventh grade year had been. I was a little hesitant of having this agency work with me because I was afraid they were going to change who I am and try to push me to do things I didn't want to do. However, I had no choice since I was an emotional train wreck that couldn't objectively make decisions for myself.

The relationship between me and the nonpublic agency therapist assigned to work with me was an ongoing battle. I was highly resistant to what she was trying to teach me. She was part of an agency whose ultimate goal was to try to make me "fit in" socially in a mainstream environment. This prevented me from cooperating with her because I thought she was going to force me to interact with my peers or push me to develop more teen interests. I have to admit I was pretty mean to her. Instead of engaging with her in a mature way, I used behavior to communicate to her that I didn't like the ideas she was trying to implement. I did things like name calling and even intentionally stepped on her foot. Perhaps the biggest thing she did that triggered me was that she started talking about my transition to high school. It was still in the middle of the school year so I didn't see the point of talking about high school prematurely. It just felt too overwhelming. In addition, the concept of transition was a huge trigger for me and I felt as though she didn't understand that this topic in particular caused me so much anxiety. One time, the therapist and I were sitting in the middle of a classroom and she started talking about making the switch to high school.

Of course this is the worst place to be talking about a trigger subject since there was a classroom full of kids. After a few minutes, I lost my temper and started shouting at her telling her I was done talking about the subject. I eventually moved myself away from her. Another therapist who was also consulting for the school but not part of the non-public agency saw what was going on and decided to chat with me. I told her my situation and how I felt that the therapist was not listening to me. She gave me the best advice. She told me in her British accent that I "should try to be the better person". This therapist really got me and I was so glad to have met her. A year later, she would be the therapist who would work with me at school.

Another issue I had with this agency was that they tried to do a little "fade-the-aide" with me in my math class before I was ready. Although at the time it didn't seem like a big deal, I realized now that this practice was pushing me way too fast and way too far. Fade the aide should be a gradual process not something that should be done cold turkey. In this situation I wasn't allowed to ask my aide to help me with my class work instead I should rely on my teacher. This caused a huge inconvenience for me because the teacher couldn't give me the attention I needed to understand the class concepts. My aide in this case knew how to do algebra so I asked her to help me anyway. The therapist told my aide that I couldn't ask her for help in my math class at all anymore. It was hard to break that cycle since I was used to asking her for help and to cut it off suddenly felt harsh. Because of this poorly done "fade-the-aide" attempt, I ended up doing the homework not being sure if I was doing it correctly.

In January of my eighth grade year my mom wanted to hire a behaviorist to work with me on emotional regulation, social skills and developing more age appropriate interests. This behaviorist was recommended by one of my mother's friends who also had a daughter on the autism spectrum. We couldn't use her right at the beginning of the year because I was so preoccupied with soccer practice and with a treatment called neurofeedback which helps people with ADHD to concentrate.

By January the soccer season was over. I also stopped going to the neurofeedback because I felt it wasn't doing anything for me. With all of this in the past I now had time to work with a behaviorist. Her name is Heather and to my surprise she was very laid back and pretty hip. She didn't remind me of a traditional therapist. However, I was very resistant to seeing another therapist. I was so fed up with the agency at school that it made me skeptical of anyone making any attempts to help me. But Heather was different from the others. For one thing, Heather came to my house instead of me going to her office. At our first session Heather promised me she wouldn't push me to do things that I wasn't ready to do or felt uncomfortable with. Heather kept her word and has continued to do so till this day. I consider her one of the best support people I've ever had. I liked the fact that Heather didn't talk at me. Also, unlike so many others Heather never treated me as though I were inferior. She was very open about her personal life and used stories from her own life to show me that just because she is a therapist doesn't mean that she doesn't have her own issues that she has to work on. Heather's approach put a more personable twist to therapy. It made me feel like I was talking to a person instead of a brick wall that is common in more traditional office-based therapy.

One tool that Heather introduced to me that helped me significantly was the mood thermometer. The mood thermometer is a visual tool that uses three colors: green, yellow and red. The colors represented my mood. Green meant a calm mood, yellow meant a little stressed out and red meant very stressed out and is usually applied to when I was having a meltdown. This tool made it very easy to understand my moods. Today, Heather and I continue to work with each other and maintain an unbreakable bond.

While going through puberty and getting ready to transition to high school, I clung to my childhood more than ever. Growing up is hard for anyone but it was especially really hard for me. From when I was little cartoon characters have been a fascination to me. Sesame Street characters, Pokémon, Nickelodeon characters, Power puff girls and Dragon ball Z were staples. The characters I was interested in would change overtime depending on my age. But one thing that remained constant was that I had to collect all the merchandise associated with my favorite characters. As I got older I started to develop an intense preoccupation with the Disney Princesses, Barbie and Hello Kitty because I couldn't face the fact that I was turning into a young woman. I also had a little cousin who was interested in those things so this helped in terms of deflection. However most of the merchandise that had my favorite characters was geared towards little girls not teenagers. This made me mad because I was thirteen years old and I still liked those friends. But society, in its ignorance, thinks that they were only appropriate for little girls. Regardless, I bought their merchandise. I bought everything from jewelry to bedding. I also wore Disney Princess t-shirts to school that resulted in me looking quite different from my peers. Luckily the school staff didn't look down on me for having these interests. They actually used it to reinforce good behavior and during Christmas and my birthday they would give me Disney Princess and Hello Kitty accessories. A lot of the stuff that girls my age were into like makeup, designer clothes and boys were too mature and intimidating for me. People tried to gently introduce me to what girls my age were into but what they didn't know was that these inanimate personas were the foundation of my comfort zone. If anyone took them away I would instantly feel dysfunctional. I knew that being into these pre-adolescent icons was not considered "age appropriate" and that it would make it hard for me to fit in with my typical peers. But I didn't care about fitting in with "typical peers" so I felt it was pointless for my parents and staff members to try to introduce me to "their" interests.

The reason why I am sharing this personal story is because for some teens and young adults with autism, cartoon characters provide joy and an escape from the hardships of growing up. Therefore I want to describe some of the challenges of trying to balance the maintenance of individuality, fitting in with society and navigating a typical school environment. Our society tends to dictate what interests and activities are appropriate for different age groups. The problem is that when we put people in categories or boxes it causes unnecessary tension and anxiety when they don't conform to society's rigid standards. Being into these harmless characters like Hello Kitty and Disney princess is part of my identity and people should respect my interests instead of treating them as a pathology or a symptom of my autism.

For friends, I preferred to hang out with the other kids who were in "special education". I didn't feel comfortable hanging out with my typical peers because I felt they couldn't personally relate to what I was going through and wouldn't understand what it's like to live with a disability. Typical peers also wouldn't be interested in some of the same things I was interested in. There was a boy who was in my adaptive physical education class that I started hanging out with during the majority of my eighth grade year. What brought us together was that we both had a desire to act silly. Like me, he would laugh at some of the same things like "potty" jokes. He also seemed really happy and unlike me he didn't let the small stuff get to him. I felt the happiest and least anxious when I was with him. We would eat lunch together with a group of the other students who also had special needs and make funny jokes about some of the people in our lives. In fact we teased the adaptive physical education teacher by calling him names and sang creative songs about him. My friend also assisted me in torturing the ABA therapist who was helping me at school. The comedic stunts that my friend and I tried to attempt sometimes got us in trouble. For instance during silent reading time, my friend and I decided to draw silly pictures of our P.E. teacher. We then started laughing instead of reading like we were suppose to so we got into trouble and I got my drawings taken away from me. Even though he was a grand source of trouble making I was sad to leave middle school because I would be leaving my friend behind since he had another year to go.

Another problem that year was my physical education class. There was a girl in my adaptive physical education class that was causing me trouble so my mom decided that I should be in a regular physical education class. I had to change my class schedule but I was lucky to keep the same teachers for my other classes. However, things in the regular physical education class weren't rosy either. The teacher that I had for P.E. was not understanding of my special needs. My poor fine motor skills prevented me from playing sports effectively. As a result I received a lower grade than my peers in P.E. since the teacher graded based on performance not effort. I found this completely unjust. I ended up hating P.E. Hard competitive sports like water polo and volleyball were the norm. I played my hardest but my ability level was just lower then what was expected. This left me truly humiliated.

Academically, eighth grade was a tough year as well. My grades sort of slipped compared to sixth and seventh grade because the subjects were really tough. In fact eighth grade was the only year I didn't make the honor roll in middle school. My English class was the one that brought down my overall GPA. The reason for this was because I had a hard time writing a five paragraph essay. I just couldn't seem to organize my writing, nor incorporate quotes into something coherent and complete. My mom tried to help make essay writing an easier task for me. We tried outlines, assistive technology and some special software where I could organize my thoughts but I showed no interest in them. In fact when a guy came to do an assessment of assistive technology for me I resisted and threw a meltdown. So I struggled for a year. As the years went on, writing is less of a challenge for me as you, the reader, can see.

Despite the emotional turmoil I was experiencing that year, one thing that alleviated my stress was art. I took ceramics and it became my favorite class of the day. I made things from coiled pots to sculptures of my favorite characters. Working with clay allowed me to use my creative side at school and have a break from hard core academics. Outside of school, I would make different comic strips to help relieve my stress. Drawing pictures was another avenue in which to express my emotions. When I was angry or stressed I would draw pictures of what was bothering me.

Unfortunately eighth grade was the year that I became the most anxious. A majority of the time, I felt anxious about how people viewed me. Until that year, I never really thought that deeply about how different I was from my peers. This strong awareness of how different I was made me question my self worth. As a result, I started asking for reassurance from people to the point where it drove them crazy. Because I had a hard time controlling my anxiety and it led me on a cycle of perseveration, I had to be on medication. I was very resistant to the idea of being medicated because I associated medication with people who were sick and I was worried it would change my personality. I was prescribed Zoloft to help me manage my stress. Zoloft helped alleviate some of my symptoms but I still continued to have anxiety. For the next three years, I went on and off my medication depending how intense the anxiety was. It wasn't until my junior year of high school, that I weaned myself off the meds. To this day, I still question my behaviors and lifestyle but not to the same degree in intensity like I did in my eighth grade year.

At the closing of my eighth grade year, we had my annual IEP which also was a transition IEP because I would be attending high school the following year. The assistant principal was not happy with the performance of the nonpublic agency since there were other students in the school district that were also having problems with them so she called the director of special education to "fire" the agency at my IEP meeting. This shocked everyone who was in attendance. That was very hard. But on a positive note the lovely British therapist that I met earlier in the year would be working with me in high school. She would be responsible for writing the behavioral support plan at school, train the aide who would be working with me and work with me directly on learning skills such as stress management and appropriate social skills.

Chapter 8

The Computer Teacher

As I close my middle school years, I'd like to reflect on a teacher who I felt very close with and managed to make my middle school years a relatively pleasant experience. This is a chapter within itself because I have learned very valuable lessons from this relationship and I want to go more in depth about why I felt so comfortable with her.

She was my computer teacher. I met her at the very beginning of my middle school career. I had her as part of my school's exploratory wheel where you take different electives and every six weeks you would rotate to different classes. As I mentioned before, I was new to the school district so I didn't know too many people. I felt lost and had a hard time making friends. This teacher was very approachable. She was the only person who made me feel welcome at school. When the six weeks were up, I felt sad that I wouldn't continue to see her anymore. As a result, I began to stand in front of her classroom door or eat near her classroom in hopes that she will recognize me and invite me in her room. On a few occasions, she invited me into her classroom to talk. When I was in her classroom, I enjoyed our talks. She wanted to get to know me more as a person which I appreciated. I've never had a teacher reach out to me like that before.

Although the relationship started off well it was beginning to have issues. The first incident occurred in February of my sixth grade year. My inclusion teacher, Ms. Chu, approached me and wanted to speak with me. She said that the teacher began to feel uncomfortable with me standing in front of her classroom. She advised me that I should focus on making peer friendships instead of pursuing my relationship with my teacher. When Ms. Chu told me this I got very upset and started crying. I thought my computer teacher was mad at me and didn't want to talk to me because she thought I

46

was stalking her. My aide, who was my biggest ally, got mad at Ms. Chu for not being considerate of my feelings. What Ms. Chu didn't realize when she gave me this piece of "advice", was that I had feelings for this teacher and I couldn't stop thinking about her. I soon learned that the teacher didn't want Ms. Chu to tell me that she was uncomfortable because she didn't want to hurt my feelings. I wished that the teacher had been honest with me instead of telling Ms. Chu because I felt we could've worked it out peacefully.

I got my second chance though when in seventh grade when we were paired up in a mentoring "guardian angel" program. I soon found out that she chose me specifically. At first I felt nervous and awkward because she had a lot of other students and I felt it was wrong that she was singling me out but at the same time I felt honored that she had chosen me over the other students since I had a huge admiration for this teacher. We then began to meet weekly. While being in the guardian angel program strengthened my relationship with my teacher, it also brought on more challenges and problems. I still felt very shy and didn't have the confidence to start a conversation with her so I would still stand in front of her classroom to get her to recognize me. My admiration for my teacher soon turned into an unhealthy fixation. Anything that didn't involve her was not of interest to me and I had the compulsion to talk about her with my parents who became tired of me bringing her up all the time. Even though my intense interest in the computer teacher brought more problems to the people who had to be around me, it actually brought me great joy and happiness. When I perseverated on this teacher, I wanted to hold on to the feeling of intense joy it brought to me. It was a coping mechanism against the complications of middle school like the workload getting more intense and having a hard time fitting in. If I didn't have this teacher in my life, I would've had an unpleasant middle school experience.

As the school year came to a close, it became clear that my relationship with my teacher was very destructive to my everyday functioning. Since summer break was around the corner my teacher asked me if I wanted to go to Disneyland over the summer. At first, I didn't know if it was ok to do activities outside of school with your teacher but I was so excited that she had offered. This meant I got to go to the "Happiest Place On Earth" with her. However, my dream trip to Disneyland with my teacher never happened. A few weeks before school ended, my teacher told me that she couldn't see me outside of school because of a school policy that was adopted due to an incident that involved a teacher and a student. I was devastated and angry because she led me to believe that this outing to Disneyland would happen during the summer and I was really looking forward to it. To have her back out at the last minute like that made the situation even worse and I felt I couldn't get over it. This incident made me start to doubt my relationship with her all over again. I began to question whether if she genuinely liked me or was she just being nice because I had autism and had a hard time fitting in with my peers. I decided it was due to the policy. Regardless the summer between seventh and eighth grade was a long and hard one because I never got to see the teacher over the break because of a "stupid" school rule.

My relationship with the computer teacher in my last year of middle school continued to be a cycle of ups and downs. I also knew that I was going to transition to high school which meant that I was going to have to say goodbye to her once and for all. This caused me so much anxiety it made my attachment to her stronger. Which, once again made her uncomfortable. One thing that changed was that I began to go into her classroom if I wanted to talk with her rather than just standing outside her door and waiting for her to recognize me. For the most part during my eighth grade year, my relationship with this teacher ran relatively smoothly with very little incident except for the fact that I was obsessed with her.

At the end of my last year of middle school, my teacher agreed that she would keep in touch with me and we would see each other over the summer. Of course I was full of excitement and beyond thrilled that she wanted to continue the relationship after I graduated middle school and I felt that nothing could go wrong with the relationship anymore since I was no longer a student there. However I soon realized that my beliefs and assumptions were proven false. It all started with me sending her way too many emails because she wasn't clear with me of how often I could contact her. The emailing started out fine but the trouble began when she didn't return some of them. I began panicking and getting anxious because I thought she was avoiding me. It wasn't until one of my behaviorists told me that the teacher was uncomfortable with me emailing her excessively. After that incident, I had come to the hard truth that my relationship with this teacher was unhealthy and it was best if I discontinue it and move on with my life. This was very difficult for me but I did it.

As I reflect on this relationship I learned some valuable lessons about boundaries and personal space. I realized that the teacher was sending me mixed messages and as a result she was making promises she couldn't keep. Because of that I felt the relationship was something it wasn't. I also was immature at the time and didn't know any better about respectful interactions with adults. I felt that the relationship started off healthy and that the teacher had good intentions but she never got the guidance she needed in dealing with students on the autism spectrum. Since there was so much trauma and emotion that was left as a result of this situation, I became very doubtful that I would have a healthy relationship with any adults in my life. This pain carried over through high school and I didn't get over it until years later. However, the positive thing that I learned from this relationship is the importance of boundaries and how they are there for personal safety internally and externally.

Chapter 9

Transitioning to High School

Once again I had to start another school transition. For a while I resented this because by now I knew that things could get very complicated very quickly. I had just gotten used to my middle school and I finally found some peers who I identified with. However, they all happened to be a year younger than myself so they had one more year to go whereas I was on my way to high school.

To get me acquainted with the new school I'd be attending in the fall, my parents and the rest of the people on my IEP team felt that I should take summer school there. I decided to take a summer reading class since it was the least demanding class offered. There I would have an aide accompany me for emotional support. We also signed up for the girls' cross-country team where I could get my exercise. However, the cross-country team required the girls to run long distances which I was not good at. I couldn't even run a mile without feeling exhausted so it was decided that I would run on the track instead before my summer class began. My aide, who was someone I was already familiar with from middle school offered to run with me. So every morning my aide and I would get up really early and run some laps. While running laps, we got closer and learned a lot about each other. I learned that my aide has a daughter who had sustained a brain injury after surgery to remove a tumor. She explained that this was the incentive to work with special needs students. After hearing that story I gained a higher level of respect for her. I knew then that she was doing this job because it was personal. She had a passion for this delicate population being that she had to deal with it firsthand every single day. This made her stand out to me above and beyond all the other aides in the district.

So, I took my summer reading class in the learning center where all the resource classes are held. The other students in my class also had various disabilities so it was not a mainstreamed class. The teacher who ran the class was really nice and I bonded with her right away. We had a lot of things in common like she happened to live across the street from my old house that I grew up in. The teaching assistant was also very friendly and had a great sense of humor. She would call me playful names like "Nosy Matilda" since I would look through the cabinet on her desk drawer. The warm and welcoming nature of both the teacher and the teaching assistant eased some of my anxiety about being a dreaded 'high school student'.

Emotionally, the class was relatively stress free except when we had to read a book about someone with autism. The book was about a boy who had autism and had savant like qualities. With these unusual gifts he tries to solve the murder of his neighbor's dog. What bothered me about this book was that it was full of stereotypes none of which described me at all. The boy in the book did have behavioral problems but one of my classmates went as far as to call him 'retarded'. My classmate's ignorant comment really angered me. I took it very personally since I suffered from the same disorder as the boy in the book. What concerns me the most is when neurotypical authors rely on second hand accounts about the autistic community. For any of the population that is uninformed about autism these stereotypes can easily lead them to believe that all persons on the spectrum are the same. This couldn't be farther from the truth. I don't know if that classmate would want to get to know me if he found out that I have the same disorder as the boy in the story. Because autism maintains such a stigma, mostly via media, I am hesitant to confide in my peers.

Fortunately, right at this time, I started working with a new behaviorist. She was the nice British woman who gave me the wise advice when I was having problems with the nonpublic agency therapist assigned to me a year earlier. Her name was Rachel and she was very outgoing and very hip. Like Heather my home behaviorist, she was very understanding and really understood the autistic mind extremely well. I used to be very silly and called her *Supernanny* because she was British and worked well with children. Luckily Rachel had a good sense of humor about it. Rachel and I met weekly at the high school after my summer reading class. We spent our sessions getting to know each other. Rachel was actually the first person to recognize that my need to jump was not a behavior. The root cause of why I had to jump was because of my overactive sensory system. Since I was little jumping has been an issue. In middle school, I used to jump all the time during lunch and nutrition breaks. People used to call me all sorts of names from "Tigger" to "Jumping bean". In fact during eighth grade, one of my IEP goals was for me to stop jumping completely. What people don't realize is that jumping calms me down and relieves my sensory urges. Rachel's insight into my jumping made me realize that I was very fortunate to have had therapists who respected my uniqueness and weren't on a mission to fix me.

During the same summer Heather was trying to get me interested in going to the mall. Back then I was not so interested in going shopping unless of course it was to add to my Hello Kitty collection. The whole intent of doing our sessions at the mall was to introduce me to the latest teen fashion trends. I hated it at first because, as I mentioned before, I was afraid to grow up and I thought that a lot of the clothing stores that teens were into were superficial. I also thought that Heather was trying to get me to conform to the rest of my peers. Eventually, I developed my sense of fashion but it wasn't until the end of my sophomore year that I finally got the hang of hitting the mall routinely.

Another trigger that came with transitioning to high school was the thought of taking on more responsibilities and developing more independence. The concept of "independence" was scary for me because it meant that I had to do things on my own without help from parents and other support people. i.e., grow up. As a result of having so much anxiety about being independent no one could even use the word around me. If in fact they did I would proceed in throwing a fit. Today, the concept of independence still triggers me but not to the same degree as it did back then.

The first few months of high school were tough. I had noticed that a lot of the female students took advantage of the more lenient dress code and their choices were provocative. In addition to girls dressing more like young women, the seniors looked more like adults and I felt that I was going to school with a bunch of college students. There were guys who already had mustaches. Seeing this made me feel very out of place as I already felt young for my age.

The academic expectations also rose in high school. There was more reading and writing and instead of a trimester system that was in place at middle school we had a semester system with finals just like a college schedule. My English class gave me the most anxiety out of all my academics. The books we covered in that class all had dark themes and it made me feel uncomfortable. One book in particular called *Lord of the Flies* was so gruesome that I had to be out of class when we read it in class. High school writing standards also took a huge leap. The papers then required a critical analysis of a book which included the use of symbolism. I would flounder on these assignments since I couldn't analyze a book let alone write a five paragraph essay explaining the overall message intended.

The English teacher I had at the time was chosen for me by my inclusion teacher who thought we would be a good match. She had been successful with other learning disabled students prior. As it turned out my inclusion teacher's instincts were wrong with this selection. My English teacher seemed very cold and strict and didn't smile at all. Every time I entered her class I always felt anxious. Some days I just wanted to be out of class because the anxiety was way too much. In addition to her lack of warmth she was a very tough grader. I would get papers and assignments back and I would get a lot of C's with a ton of feedback explaining in detail what was wrong with my responses. Midway through the semester, we decided to switch English teachers. This new teacher and I turned out to be very compatible. She helped me improve my writing by sitting with me privately and going over my past writing assignments and taught me how to incorporate quotes from the readings into my essays. Ever since then I've been able to write a five paragraph any day.

During my first year of high school, I decided to be a little bit mischievous. Transitioning to high school was tough but that didn't stop me from having a little fun along the way. On Halloween, when everyone dressed in their costumes one of my male aides and I decided to come up with the clever idea to use a huge cardboard box and make it into a costume and walk right into my English class. However, it backfired and I got a lecture from my inclusion teacher on appropriate behavior. I also did other crazy things like put thumb tacks on my aide's chair because I saw it on TV or made a funny comic that was a parody of Romeo and Juliet that contained some inappropriate content that I care not to mention. Even though my intentions were to be funny, I got into trouble with my aide and teacher because to them I was being reckless. Having a diagnosis of autism and being in special education has put me under a microscope in terms of my behavior. I felt I was being scrutinized by people on my support team on everything from wearing character clothing to school to being way too silly. This caused me a lot of frustration since I thought my creative personality was being stifled by the strict structure of school.

Chapter 10

Me and my autism. Coming to terms with my diagnosis

Throughout my high school years, I began the process of trying to accept my autism. However, the journey to acceptance was not easy especially when attending a high school full of typically developing peers let alone the angst of being a teenager. Through this attempt I experienced feelings of inferiority and tried everything to act like and fit in with my peers.

In November 2006, there was an article in *Newsweek* magazine that talked about autism. It was titled "Autism: What Happens When They Grow Up". It talked about some of the challenges that often face teens and young adults on the autism spectrum. My mom happened to be interviewed for this article along with other families. However, we weren't sure if the interview would be mentioned in the article. My mom told the interviewer that even though I am 14-years-old and attend a regular high school and take regular general education classes, I had a hard time fitting in with my peers because I had "child-like" interests. When I entered high school not much had really changed for me since 8th grade. My mother also said in the interview that I knew that my tendencies were immature. As a result I grew paranoid and kept asking my mother incessantly if having these interests was ok for my age. At first, I was excited about the possibility that I would be mentioned in a major magazine and people would recognize me. When the article came out, both my mom and I were shocked that this possibility had become a reality. However, when I read the article my positive attitude of enthusiasm and stardom turned into humiliation. The way the article was written gave me the impression that I was a challenging case for my mom because I kept perseverating and it showed my obsessive-compulsive tendencies. It never mentioned any of my strengths or positive qualities. What bothered me the most about this article was the fact that almost the whole country now knows about my obsession with cartoon characters. I felt that my sense of privacy was violated because one of the biggest secrets I was trying to keep from the world now is public. Years later, I found this excerpt about me in a book that deals with autism which is when I realized that since this information is public it can appear in secondary sources without me ever knowing it. As a result of this article, I felt ashamed about having autism and began to feel inferior to those without. I hate it when the media portrays those with autism as being just a helpless challenge. A lot of articles written about autism only include the points of views of parents insinuating that we could not advocate for ourselves. Clearly that is not the case here.

To illustrate this point I went to a high school that was known for being competitive. Although it was public I felt that my school had the same academic expectations and rigors as any private school. Most of the students were very athletic and were involved in at least one of the school's sports teams as well as other extracurricular activities. One particular activity that a lot of students in my school were involved with was Model United Nations which was a debate club. However, the tough academic environment began to have an emotional toll on me especially during my freshman year. Even though I did well (to my surprise) academically during my first semester, I began to feel frustrated with the amount of work that was required of me. As a result, I felt that the quality of my work could never compete with theirs because of my syndrome. This feeling was especially apparent in my new English class. As I mentioned I really liked my teacher but I was also in a class full of students who were "brainiacs". I got this impression because I noticed that they kept getting A's on all their writing assignments while all I could pull off were B's. To many it may seem like I am exaggerating but I felt that I was "dumb" compared to my classmates and this thought began to dominate my thinking. This destructive thought was exacerbated when the teacher passed around a sign up sheet for accelerated English for the following year. When I received the sheet, I noticed that a majority of my classmates had signed it so I felt obligated to do the same. After class, my aide and my teacher approached me and asked if I signed the sheet out of thoughtful consideration or if I did it out of peer pressure. They thought it was not a good idea for me to take honors English because of the rigorous coursework that was assigned and the school staff didn't think I had enough coping strategies to deal with its demands. However, I didn't have the guts to tell them my true feelings that I felt inferior to the other students and I felt that signing up for honors classes would make me less likely to stick out. In the long run I'm glad the school staff talked me out of it because, to say the least, I think the stress of it all would have gotten the best of me. Another way I decided to express my feelings of inferior was to act like Holden Caulfield from *Catcher in the Rye*. In a way, I felt I could relate to Holden even though he didn't have autism. Like me, Holden had a hard time fitting into mainstream society and figuring out how it operates. Unfortunately for the people who had to deal with me, the Holden Caulfield persona I decided to portray increased my use of foul language. Until then I never cussed because I felt it was wrong. It seemed for the next couple of months every other word that came out of my mouth was the F-word or the God***** expletive. Of course, as always, I got reprimanded for taking on this vernacular because it was slightly unsuitable. Luckily, this phase was only temporary and I was able to resume my normal life once I felt more comfortable in my skin.

As a result of the frustration I had at school from feeling different from the other students, my mom grew concerned and started to question if being in a regular school was the right placement for me. This prompted her in searching for other options like a private special education school. One school she thought was a good candidate had a program for pupils on the autism spectrum. For some odd reason I wanted to stay at my home school since I felt that going to a "special school" was a sign of failure because I couldn't handle myself in a typical school environment. In the end, everyone thought it was best that I stayed at my regular high school since I had a wonderful behaviorist and I was clearly blossoming.

In high school, I began to read about autism to learn more about myself and to try to see if anything in them could be applied to my life. I had always read my mom's autism books because they were convenient. To my dismay, a lot of the books that my mom had were written by parents and professionals. There weren't too many books written by individuals who had autism so there was no one to represent me. What's worse is that parents and professionals rely on stereotypes to describe autism. Examples of these cop outs that I personally found offensive was that we lacked empathy and no sense of humor. Neither of these characteristics had anything to do with me. I'm extremely empathetic and have a wacky sense of humor. The distortions in perspective between individuals who have autism and neurotypical parents and experts has given me the motivation to one day to become a autism self-advocate so I can prove these stereotypes wrong. It also gets me when the autism experts suggest that "normalization" will lead us to happier lives. For some individuals maybe this is the case but it certainly wasn't the case for me. As I illustrated, during my middle school years and for many years to follow I have faced enormous anxiety and conflict in trying to become 'normal'. But, in doing so I had to conceal parts of my true self. This is where my true internal struggle took root.

Chapter 11

Sophomore Year Madness

The summer of 2007 was a peaceful one after having a stressful and tumultuous freshman experience. Being that I didn't go to summer school that year I had a lot of free time on my hands. Some of it was spent on walks around my neighborhood to get some exercise and to clear my mind. The rest of it was spent in two autism camps that summer. One was a day camp and the other was a sleep away camp. The day camp I went to had all boys. I was literally the only girl in the group. Even the therapist who ran the camp was male. The only people who were female in the camp were the volunteers. The uneven gender ratio is a common reminder that autism is a disorder that primarily strikes boys more than girls. While being in a group with a bunch of boys didn't bother me as much when I was younger, I now felt removed from them because their interests were entirely different from my own. They were drawn to video games and violence wherein I found both to be simply nightmare inducing.

The sleep away camp I went to was a surprisingly better experience. At first, I was a little hesitant going to an overnight camp because I've never been away from home before and new places scare me. However, once I got there my anxious mindset began to change when I met other girls there and we immediately clicked. The other cool part about this camp was that we stayed in college dorms on the UCLA campus and ate in the dining halls which gave me a sense of what college is about. I had a blast during my week at that camp and I was really sad to leave.

When school resumed in the fall I was not excited about going back to hitting the books. I braced myself. However, it was the homework load I never saw coming. I had to add another class to my schedule making it now containing a total of four academic classes. The amount of assigned work we were to do at home was off the charts.

Another weighty thing that was going on in my life as I was readjusting back to school was that my other grandfather was starting to fall ill. During the summer his cancer had return after having been in remission for five months. Although he was fine during the summer, come fall his radiation treatment began and with that his energy waned. This became unavoidably noticeable when he began to show no interest in golfing. This was alarming because for his entire life being referred to as an avid golfer was an understatement. Seeing my grandfather in a seemingly weak state reminded me of what happened to my other grandfather three years ago when he lost his balance and fell down. I had that same feeling of doom that my grandpa was going to die really soon. After that experience, I would keep asking my parents if it was true. They would try to assure me "no, grandpa wasn't going to die" but I could tell from their expression that they weren't being completely truthful with me since they didn't want me to get distracted from my studies. It wasn't until the seventh day of October, that my worst nightmare came true. When I came back from school, my parents broke the sad news to me that my grandfather has passed away. After receiving the news, I felt confused and had the feeling that what had just happened was unreal because I remembered a few months ago that he was alive and well and now he was dead. However, the sadness and grief did not come out until his funeral. I started crying because he was my last grandfather and now I have no grandfathers in my life that I can visit and spend time with. However, I didn't experience regret when he died like I did with my first grandfather. I felt that I fully appreciated the times and memories I spent with him. One fond memory that I had with him was eight months before his death. We were in a supermarket together and he took me to the dessert aisle. My grandpa had a sweet tooth and would use his grandchildren as a pawn to help him buy a garden variety of his favorites. He asked me which one of the desserts I would like to eat. I chose a chocolate donut while he settled for a plain glazed. I know it seems pretty trivial but it was one of my favorite memories that we had together since it was just me and him and we were being naughty. After he passed a void in my heart began to grow and I felt no end in sight.

In addition, I ended up with the most anal retentive and obsessive-compulsive history teacher ever! He would have ridiculous and unrealistic expectations. For instance he wanted all the students to have a specific type of folder that was hard to find in stores. He sold it in class for 25 cents each which I thought he was taking advantage of the students by making a profit off of us. In rebellion, I refused to get the folder because I didn't want to give my teacher any of my money. But my aide went ahead and made the black market purchase so I was kind of forced to get the folder. Adding insult to injury the homework I got from that class took over an hour to complete. It could've taken less time if my teacher didn't have this ludicrous format which involved organizing my notes into headings, subheadings, key points, etc. Being in that class caused so much anxiety that I would come home everyday from school and just vent. In short order my parents began to get a tad sick of hearing about him ad-nauseam. In fact, my dad said sarcastically that it felt like my history teacher has moved into our house.

Things intensified during the second semester when he assigned a big research paper. The paper had to be in a certain format and he was very nitpicky about the line margins having to be a certain inch or he would knock off points. In addition, we had to do extra stuff for the paper including making flash cards illustrating our sources, outlines etc. I remember doing the flash cards and it took over three hours to complete on a Saturday no less! After all the hard work I did, my teacher approached me and told me that he wasn't going to give me any points for the flash cards since I didn't do it in the format he wanted. He could've given me partial credit but my history teacher was an "all or nothing" kind of guy. After the flashcards incident I lost my temper and I stormed out of class once the bell rang for lunchtime. I was so pissed off that I left without waiting for my aide and she had to go look for me.

The school staff and my parents tried everything to alleviate the intense stress and anxiety I had towards his relentless research project. My behaviorist Rachel developed a time management template in which I could break down the project into smaller pieces. I would sit either with my aide or my inclusion teacher and we would go over the steps that would be needed to complete it. It helped somewhat but my angst was so intense every time the subject was brought up that I would go into the red or yellow zone in no time. Then my inclusion teacher offered to have her son come over and help with the organization process. As a result writing the paper became easier. Regardless my anxiety was rooted and was beginning to drive my parents and school staff a bit nuts. When the paper was over and after I turned it in, my state of mind began to mellow a bit but I felt so worn out that for next year I wanted to take a slower paced history class instead of a college prep class. I was also very insistent that I didn't get the same teacher again for both my junior and senior year.

Another class I had a hunch that might be tad challenging was geometry. My parents verified this notion my telling me just how hard geometry was before I began the class. But, once again, my parents were telling it like it was. Saying that I had a hard time understanding the concepts with its theorems, lines and angles was just a tad of an understatement. Let's just say I couldn't attempt to touch the homework unless I was helped by my aide who understood how to do math. When it was test time, I felt the problems were new to me even though we covered the concepts in class. As a result of not knowing how to solve most of the problems I got C's on most of my tests. This added fuel to my "anxiety fire" and lowered my confidence. I hated getting C's since I usually get A's and B's in all my other classes. It's been decided that I am more of an algebraic equation type of girl than a geometric girl with all its lines and angles.

Sophomore year was a school year I would rather forget. It was the hardest year yet. I guess it makes sense that it would be but at the time the increasing work load always came as a shock. I also had to deal with aftermath of emotions that came as a result of my grandfather's death only months prior. But it appeared that the worst was over. Luckily, for the rest of my school career that was the last of my academically over the top school years ever again.

Chapter 12

Discovering Myself

My junior year of high school was when I really started the journey of self discovery. Most of my peers started this rite of passage much earlier than me but because I had a lot of issues that I had to deal with I started this process at sixteen years old. Junior year was the year that I began to come out of isolation and began to talk to both peers and adults.

This also happened to be the time I started showing an interest in fashion. As mentioned earlier Heather had always been trying to build up my fashion sense. However, after all her hard work I finally developed an interest in going shopping on my own time. I started becoming interested in some of the stores teens my age were into such as Forever 21 and H&M as well as a few expensive brands such as Juicy Couture and True Religion. Unfortunately, my new interest in fashion turned into an unhealthy obsession with jean sizes. I remembered trying on a pair of jeans and it felt very tight on me and as a result I felt insecure about my weight. My insecurity was exacerbated by the fact that the girls at my school were super skinny. As a result I would skip lunch at school so I can make myself thinner.

This, however, didn't last very long. The school staff began to become concerned about me because they were afraid I was going to develop an eating disorder. Rachel had to step in and told me that what I was doing was very unhealthy. I finally began eating lunch again.

At about this same time I began to resent the increased expectations that people had placed on me as a result of not having an aide for the first time since first grade.

I found it very hard in the beginning since I was now responsible for keeping track of homework assignments and talking to teachers about my needs. So there I was on my own and my old aide was working with a friend of mine who had a physical disability. As a result I felt resentful and irrationally jealous. I actually made comments to my previous aide and teacher that I wanted to be more severely disabled like my friend so I would have the support I felt I still needed. It took a lot of therapy sessions to process my feelings about this issue since there were a lot of layers to uncover. I finally learned that I should be grateful for my abilities since people who are physically disabled have frustrations as a result of depending on someone to do even little things for them.

I believe that this therapy caused an intellectual and emotional growth spurt. I started working on the skill of self advocacy in my junior year. Before I was able to advocate for myself, my parents would make all the decisions for me and I had no voice. This was all new territory for me and I found it difficult from the get go. Over time, I finally realized how empowering it was to self-advocate that my opinions mattered and were well worthy of being heard. As a result of having this new ability, I can now decide on who my friends are, what college I will attend after high school and even choose the people who support me.

Saying no to people had always been extremely difficult for me especially with people I care about because I didn't want to hurt their feelings or be labeled as inflexible or close-minded.

However, if I say yes all the time I will not be respected as an individual. I want to be my own person who has a voice of her own. My behaviorist is currently helping me find it and making sure it's heard. Learning self-advocacy and finding a voice is the one thing I recommend that all people on the spectrum should learn before they approach adulthood.

I started to ask the question whether certain behaviors and viewpoints are the result of having autism or if it was part of my unique personality. Whenever I have a need, want or behavior that is different from other people my age, I automatically think it is related to being on the spectrum. It gets confusing at times because my typical peers tend to be pretty closed off when it comes anything personal, whereas I lean towards being more expressive. An example I can give from my own life that demonstrates this conflict is that I tend to gravitate towards maternal figures. I know that most teenagers don't want someone around who is very motherly and I feel that my need somehow relates to being autistic. As a result I sometimes feel immature because of it. Autism can play some part in it being that I need very patient and accepting people in my life and they just tend to be women, but not all. Professionals should be careful when deciding if a behavior is part of one's autism or is it part of that unique individual. Perhaps the most difficult part of trying to maintain this individual identity is disagreeing with your parents. My parents especially my mom is for the most part are pretty supportive. However, I had a few times when I had arguments with my mom especially over clothing choices. I love my mom very much and I hate to disappoint her. As a result, I would keep asking her permission if it's ok to have these feelings. At the same time, I feel like I have to hold back my opinions and viewpoints in order to please her.

Even though there are times my mom says things that really hurt my feelings because sometimes she doesn't think before she says things. I know the reason my mom does this is because she loves me and wants the best possible life for me. As much as I appreciate that I also need her to know that I am old enough to start making decisions for myself and that I have my own way of doing things.

Gender identity became somewhat important in high school. I was really sensitive about if people viewed me as being girly since one of the stereotypes of girls on the autism spectrum is they have a hard time being feminine. When I was in elementary school, I wanted to be a tomboy and insisted that everyone called me "Chris". Over the years I've wanted to have more of a feminine identity. I grew my hair longer and tried to act like a "girly girl". The thing that bothered me the most was having a low pitched voice. I felt that having a low pitch voice wasn't feminine enough and as a result I was nervous talking on the phone. Of course there are things of the traditional feminine identity that I decided not to adopt like wearing makeup and being "boy crazy" since I feel those things are personally over the top. While I decided to take on a more feminine identity some girls on the autism spectrum might prefer to be tomboys and enjoy traditional masculine activities. Regardless, it is all about personal freedom.

Chapter 13

Navigating Complicated High School Friendships

For most of my life, making friends with my same age peer group has been hard, and admittedly, on the verge of becoming thematic. That being said, I'm taking on this chapter with a more introspective approach. One that focuses predominantly on my internal struggles as opposed to external and environmental influences. For starters I attended high school in a well to do beach community. Most of the students in attendance had parents who would pamper them with lots of money, designer clothes and cars. Like a Lexus at sixteen. Yes, that kind of pampering. This particular high school environment did not reflect the diversified socioeconomics of the population by any stretch, especially not mine. And, as expected, my classmates' expensive tastes made it very hard to compete. It seems that you have to either come from a family with a lot of money or have a personal trait that makes you admirable among the other students in order to score a lot of friends. Truth be told, I had neither. It also didn't help that most of the people who attended my high school were white whereas I was one of the few Asian Americans. Another part of this separation had something to do with this unspoken dress code that I wasn't privy to. It was as though I never got the memo. More perplexing and isolating still was that they all dressed the same. I actually found it sad that all individuality was erased in exchange for 'high fashion', aka: 'Cool'.

This was also a time where there were a lot of parties and upsettingly, underage drinking. I'm sure it happens at every high school but it became such a problem that my school started a special program just to address the issue as well as other issues that face high school students. I felt even more alone. Even if what they were doing was destructive and held absolutely no appeal to me whatsoever.

So, let's just say that I felt a tad peer group 'light'. I tried sitting at lunch with some established cliques at the urging of my support team. But, I found it very difficult to get involved in the conversation the group was having since it was unstructured and people were talking over each other making what they were saying extremely hard to follow. I didn't know when it was appropriate to join in the conversation and as a result I felt lost. In addition it seemed that the members of these cliques knew each other for a very long time whereas I was a newbie. As a result, as ruthless as teen girls can be, I was often ignored. To be honest, I didn't really have any interest in being part of a group or to 'fit in' with anyone in my age group for that matter. I only engaged in these activities because my mom and my support team pushed me to be more social. They, the A-Team, had a plan. My mission was to find friends and they suggested that I explore school clubs. This was not only a suggestion. This was a goal on my I.E.P.! So, of course, I went for it.

Unfortunately, what stands out for me the most is the feeling of complete overwhelm. I became resistant. Clubs mean groups of people and groups of people don't work for me! Trying to even decipher who I wanted to try to start a conversation with caused me such anxiety I couldn't have even told you what club I had joined.

Later, when talking to Heather I realized that the reason why I was so resistant to the idea of joining these mini-establishments was because I was afraid that my peers would see my autism without me being aware of it and as a result judge me. My support team is not in my body so they don't realize how much extra effort I have to put in *all* social interactions. To me it perpetually feels like I'm doing a double shift. I understood their reasoning. I know the importance of being socialized and all that but the truth is, as counterintuitive as it may seem, as a teen I preferred the company of adults. I felt safer with them. In their presence, I felt my socialite prowess rise. I preferred this demographic for several reasons. For one, I found the topics of their conversations infinitely more interesting. Secondly, I knew that they were beyond the pre-judgment stupor teens seem to be steeped in. My diagnosis no longer felt open to misinterpretation. But even this preference felt open to evaluation from *someone*. Now I felt insecure about it. Being that having difficulty relating to peers is the hallmark symptom of autism, somewhere, someone, somehow was going to call me out. However, in my defense, there are other factors that influenced my preferences that came into play. Like, being an only child and going to years of therapy as well as other situations where adult involvement was required. While the circumstances might have prevented me from relating very well to peers, I felt that the intensive adult intervention was crucial in my development.

To get the experience and to have somewhat of a normal social life at school, we decided to find some nice high school girls who could act as 'peer mentors.' I was part of a school club where typically developing teens hang out with students with special needs. There were a couple of girls that I bonded with at the club.

My mom then talked with the program coordinator to ask the girls if they would be interested in being my "buddies" and hanging with me outside of school. Luckily they were. So, we would hang out on certain days after school and do small activities like going to get frozen yogurt, walk by the beach, going to see movies and go shopping. In the beginning, the outings were consistent and I felt happy spending time with them. I felt like a typical high school student doing typical high school things. In my mind I considered these girls to be my "friends" since they were the same age and we actually had fun. However the circumstances started to change especially during my junior year. All of the sudden the girls started canceling out on me and not returning calls nor texts. It was like all of a sudden the girls went M.I.A. I felt really hurt. At first, I blamed myself because I felt the reason why they didn't want to be with me anymore was because they thought I was boring or no fun. Or it was because they had busy schedules and it was poor planning on their part. Studies show though that peer mentors are helpful as long as the so-called peer 'buddy' becomes one. The disadvantage is that everyone is so close in age, the boundaries between friend and mentor are blurred. Therefore misunderstandings could result, and they did. I'm not a fan. These types of relationships are usually not genuine nor long lasting because they're somewhat forced. The people who actually *were* there for me, consistently, in high school were my two behaviorists and my aide whom I will be discussing in the next chapter.

Chapter 14

The Wonderful Aide in High School

As I've referenced, from the first grade, I had a one-to-one aide who would help me out every day at school. She would accompany me to my classes and would make sure I would stay on task during class time as well as modeling appropriate social behavior. Over the years aides would change along with my academic transitioning. However, it wasn't until high school that our relationships became very pivotal in my life. This one aide, Kathy, became vital for me to successfully get through those years. Some parents and professionals have negative views on aide relationships because they often result in dependency and therefore a marked lack of progress.

The first time I met my aide Kathy was my first day of high school. Before meeting me, however, she had reservations about working with me because she read my IEP files. Files that demonstrated a huge span of disruptive behaviors that she was going to have to monitor. Fortunately for me when we met in person, she explained later, a fair amount of her ambivalence faded. Apparently, upon introduction, she realized that perhaps I wasn't the she-devil as had been portrayed on paper. All I had to do was look her in the eye to know she was kind. I knew right then that we were going to get along and that I would be safe.

What made her distinguishable from the other aides at school was her southern drawl. I was so fascinated with the way she spoke that I started impersonating her accent and pestering her about "fried chicken". She tolerated this with good humor. She also had two daughters that I would see her interact with from time to time so I knew she wasn't completely green. Being kind and a good mother, however, did not make her a pushover.

Unlike my previous aides who were pretty lenient, Kathy was very strict with me and made sure I was acting appropriately at all times. For instance, anytime I was talking about toilet humor or acting really silly in class Kathy would pull me aside and lecture me about "appropriate" behavior. She would also report my behavior to Rachel when we had our weekly meetings. That was bad enough but the thing that really made me resentful was the communication diary she kept. She would write to my mom about whatever happened at school that day. You know, meltdowns, hiding homework, the norms. I was pissed off because I felt betrayed. To express my rebellion against Kathy I would talk back and manipulate her by doing things I knew I wasn't supposed to do, like vandalizing the communication diary with pictures. This was all to get a reaction, of course. As one might expect I took the rebellion just a tad too far. Far enough for the inclusion teacher to pull me aside and give me a lecture on respect. I guess some of it sank in because by the middle of the year I began to warm up to Kathy. I began to see her nurturing side. This was the beginning of a friendship bond that was full of happiness and a growing sense of security.

For my sophomore and junior year, I was able to have lunch with Kathy one day a week. It was a privilege that I earned as a result of learning to become more independent.

Apparently I demonstrated that I was able to have a healthy relationship with her without crossing any boundaries. I looked forward to our weekly lunches since I got to talk to her about anything I wanted that wasn't school related. We got to know each other better and as a result we developed a strong bond. Not only did we talk about fun things during our lunches together but also personal things that I didn't feel comfortable talking to my mom about. She would offer me advice. Lunch time with Kathy was a reprieve from the stress that I encountered on a day to day basis.

During sophomore year, it was decided that I would work on fading Kathy as my aide so I could be independent in the classroom. This, once again, caused me to be insecure about what role Kathy would play in my life. I felt like I was having separation anxiety from her. I became so paranoid that my relationship with Kathy was going to become unhealthy that I would keep asking her for reassurance. I kept asking her if I was acting okay. She said she would tell me if I started to go overboard since we had that kind of relationship where she could be honest with me. This was beginning to be a pattern. My behaviorist Rachel stepped in at this point and suggested that perhaps Kathy's role should go from aide to mentor. Good call. This way Kathy could still be in my life and continue to support me at school. That was great but I was still going to be sad when I graduate high school because I wouldn't see Kathy as much . . . and I know replacing her in college would be no easy task.

Chapter 15

Preparing for life after High School

With all the separations and newness thinking about life after high school became rather daunting. I tried to avoid it at all costs. No one could bring the subject up with me. If they did I would get so filled with anxiety that I felt like my head would spin off my neck like a top. That being said, senior year was approaching and I couldn't stall any longer. It was time to start planning and considering all my postsecondary options.

During my annual IEP meeting in May 2009, my IEP team started drafting the goals for next year. I always hated these meetings because I would have to hear about all the areas where I needed improvement. This particular meeting however had caused a lot of anticipatory angst because now the base date expectations were already in place. These goals were all based on me performing some task and then getting rated on how well I did. The issues addressed were the areas which trigger me the most: independence goals and transitioning from high school to college. I had to try to keep myself calm during the meeting but my observant behaviorist Rachel knew by looking at my facial expression that I was anxious. Apparently, it wasn't subtle. So, back to the demands. Topping this list was that I had to start making my own doctor's appointments. This one little goal stressed me out so entirely that my levels rose from green to yellow on a dime. Clearly learning how to schedule your own doctor appointments is an important skill to learn for adulthood. I get that. But for me it was like demanding a prompt PhD.

Just to be clear; two of the things that throw me the farthest are speaking to strangers and speaking over the phone. I hit the jack pot on this one. No assistance. All independence. One would think that the importance of these IEP goals, learning the skills, is self-evident and therefore need not be discussed ad-nauseum. Not so much. It's the difficulties in performing the actual tasks that should *at least* be acknowledged. This was not the case. At this particular juncture, right there and then, I knew that the last year of high school was going to be a long one.

Leaping ahead, I knew college was in my future but I didn't want to go to a four-year-university right out of high school. I didn't want to deal with the stress of taking the SAT's and filling out college applications and living away from home in a dormitory with a roommate. I decided to take the community college route so I could take college classes while still living at home. Eventually I would transfer to a four year university but I felt that I wasn't emotionally ready to leave home just yet. During my senior year, I went to look at three different two-year colleges. One was close by. A community college just fifteen minutes from my house. The second one was a private two year college and it is also nearby but, being that it topped a hill and I do not yet drive, the commuting challenge proved unnecessary. The third college I considered was another community college that was located in Santa Monica which meant an hour commute. The choice then became clear. Short commute. Close to home. Perfect.

So, back to another tough transition. It wasn't only what I was facing that caused me duress it was as much what I was leaving . . . and that was the public high school system and all the services they provided. For the last twelve years of my life, I was surrounded by caring aides and other staff members who helped me to be successful at school.

They also provided emotional support at times when I needed it most. On the one hand I was proud of my new found independence and on the other afraid of what it actually meant to have it. Academically, my grades were excellent and I was ready to move on to the college level. Emotionally, I still needed a few extra years of high school. I know that you can stay in the school system until the age of 22. But, I felt that if I stayed in high school an extra year I would become restless since I had met all the academic requirements needed to graduate. It was a very hard decision to make since my emotional readiness and academic readiness were at odds. I knew that once I entered the college environment I would have to try extra hard to hold it together.

During my senior year I decided to get some part time work experience. There was a lady who worked at my school who was the coordinator of a program that placed high school students with disabilities in job internships. So my support team and I talked about finding an internship that would fit. I expressed that I wanted to work in a retail store that sells clothes since I was now into fashion. The coordinator tried to find a job that matched my preferences. She found two jobs: working in a shoe store or a department store. I decided to choose the department store because of the variety. Even though I wasn't a direct employee of the store, I still had to meet with the manager and do an interview. I was enthusiastic about the job and getting work experience. Over time however I realized that the job was not what I expected. It turned out to be a very unstructured environment. The first day I had to find my own way without any support or direction whatsoever.

In addition the manager wasn't around all the time on the days I worked and since I was only a paid intern and not an employee, I had no name tag to distinguish me from a regular customer. Every time I clocked in for my shift, I had to explain to an employee that I am an intern and I needed them to contact one of the managers or a supervisor to assign me a work station. It was very hard for me since the employees were not clued in that there were a couple of high school students interning at their store. It was like starting new every day. It was a chaotic six week endeavor. After this painful indoctrination it was clear to me that there needs to be more structure in these types of programs and a job coach to help navigate the workplace to ensure successful work experience.

Another coming of age experience that I went through during my senior year of high school was turning eighteen in March 2010. Many of my classmates were excited about turning eighteen years old since that would bring them a lot of freedom. However, for me, it was a stressful time since for the last seventeen years of my life I depended on my parents and actually wanted to. Now that I am considered a legal adult, I can make decisions without consultation. I get that and on the one hand I like it. But again it's that freedom vs expectation quandary that trips me up every time. I guess I took the independence concept a little too far because I suddenly found myself thinking that now I could never ask for help again. In time, however, I learned that just because you are considered a legal adult that doesn't mean you're completely cut off from being lent a helping hand from time to time.

So, even though my senior year was full of preparation and hoops in which to jump, there were some high points as well. My behaviorist Rachel gave me the opportunity to speak to parents within the school district about my experience living with autism. This was the first time I was given a chance to put my voice out there. I had a lot of experience going through the school system and living with the diagnosis for the last 18 years of my life that I felt I had quite a bit to offer. Rachel and I spent our sessions together preparing for the presentation which even included a PowerPoint! The topics I chose to discuss were about stress management techniques, sensory issues, peer friendships, aide relationships and choosing and selecting support staff as well as my good old friend 'transition'. I chose these particular topics because they were important to me at the time and had therefore gained a degree of insight. When the day of the presentation finally came, I felt nervous at first because I never really spoke in front of a large crowd of parents before. However, after taking a few deep breaths with Rachel I started to feel calm and more confident. The final product turned out great and the parents were impressed on how far I have come in my development. In fact I did two additional presentations after that one I did for Rachel. I did one for special education teachers and for school psychologists. Doing presentations has boosted my confidence in speaking in front of a large group of people and it was also the dawning of my career as a self-advocate.

In addition to doing presentations, I was nominated for a scholar award by the special education department. At the end of each school year, my school holds an all awards assembly in which a select number of seniors as well as some juniors and sophomores are selected by each academic department. At the same time they announce the student of the year as well as the valedictorians. Each of the nominees names would be called in front of the entire school but only one of them would get the department award. Even though I didn't get the award, I was honored to have been one of the chosen few since only about 30-40 students are nominated each year.

In June 2010, I graduated from high school with a diploma with an overall GPA of 3.7. Graduation was a bittersweet moment as I reflected on the last four years and how I made the most progress both on an emotional and social level. I remembered at the beginning of my freshman year I wasn't sure how well I was going to do or even survive going to a public school. However, with the support from my aide Kathy, my two behaviorists Heather and Rachel and of course my loving parents, I was able to thrive.

Chapter 16

My first year of College

In the fall of 2010, I started at my new community college. I've never felt that college would come so soon but it did. College transitioning is probably the hardest for people living with an ASD because of the entire decision making process and the radical night and day change from those dear old high school days. This was the big step, stepping into the real world, my world. The world of college.

My choice was a junior college. As I said before, the reason I decided on this going there was because I didn't want to deal with the stress of the admissions process. I also didn't want to take the SATs and the ACT. My mom thought going to a community college was the best choice for me because she felt a four year university leap might be a bit far for a first step.

My first year of college went off without a hitch. In my first semester I took two elective classes and one academic class so I could get use to the routine as well as campus life. It was a pretty easy schedule as I didn't have too much homework. I got straight A's that semester. For the spring semester, I took an English class, a psychology class, a Spanish class and an adaptive yoga class. I was a little worried about taking Spanish since I didn't take it in high school.

So, I got a tutor to help me with homework and what do you know, I got a 4.0. Straight A's in all my classes!

College is so much different from high school. Even with the academic success, the emotional challenges of college life were extremely challenging. In high school everything was taken care of and I felt I had a safety blanket around me. I didn't have to do anything on my own since I had a shadow aide with me who I could depend on. If I was having a bad day there was always someone there that I trusted, that I knew would understand me. I also didn't have to face the task of talking with teachers about my autism since a copy of my IEP was provided. In college it's more bureaucratic and impersonal. Plus you have to ask for your own accommodations. There is more paperwork to fill out whereas in high school the only paperwork there was my IEP. In college you have to provide your own documentation and verify that you have a disability. Even if you get into your college disability center they don't provide a lot of support. Most of these centers are more equipped in dealing with learning disabilities, and physical disabilities but not for those with autism. As it had proven to be in the past, academics wasn't the problem. I needed more emotional support and someone to help me transition and get use to the whole college experience. As I mentioned earlier, students had to request their own accommodations. What I didn't mention was what a tedious process it turned out to be. You have to run to all these offices to get different signatures from different people and you must get this all done a few days before the exam or you won't get what you need most.

Based on these vast differences between college and high school, I knew that I was now in the real world.

As far as the social aspect goes making friends in college made socializing in high school look easy. I go to a community college so people usually go to class and go home. There are clubs on campus but there aren't any clubs that I'm really interested in. I did check out the psychology club at my school but there wasn't any opportunity where I could interact with the other members in the club since they always had guest speakers or a planned activity. Another social barrier I faced as a college student was finding other students with autism or any other disabilities. In high school, it was easy to find other students with special needs to identify with and they made up part of my social network. Now, because of the strict confidentiality laws about disclosure once you leave the school system, it is hard to find other students sharing in your same difficulties. As a result my feelings of isolation grew.

One enpowering aspect however was that I got to choose which professors I would disclose my disability to. This was the upside of the 'strict confidentiality laws'.

I've had professors who I felt comfortable about disclosing my autism, while others I decided it wasn't worth it. Some factors I take into consideration is if the class is going to be a challenge or if the professor has a nice personality. The reason why I am afraid to tell some professors about my disability is because I feel it wouldn't make a difference or they wouldn't understand and would think I'm using autism as an excuse.

Some professors just don't get it and their attitude might be "well you seem like you're high functioning and very capable so you should be dealing with the coursework like everyone else." I was also afraid that I would be treated as less capable and therefore differently from the other college students.

So, I only took three academic classes per semester because I know that was the limit. Some students at my college take five classes per semester which to me seems unnecessarily overwhelming. If I took five or six classes all I would do is homework and I would not have enough free time to do the things I love doing. When planning my classes, I considered how long I wanted to be at school, how hard the subjects were and how much homework they require. I also wanted to only attend class four days a week instead of five because I need that additional day off to recuperate.

This power of choice was empowering but on the other hand I have to control my autism more because college is not as forgiving as high school. I don't want students to notice the behaviors that come with my disorder. I'm afraid if they did they would automatically judge me as being "weird" or even "psychotic." There are times when I still have the urge to jump up and down while I'm on campus. However, because I have now learned when it's appropriate, I have better control of my compulsion. If I'm feeling anxious I now try to self soothe because I really don't want to make a scene. So far, I have never had a red zone at school because I was taught various strategies to deal with my anxiety.

When I come home from school, I take my "mask" off and act like myself. There, I relieve my anxiety and tension by jumping up and down and flapping my hands.

Although I am doing well in college it's not always easy to get the courses I want. At my college and at other public community colleges and universities, classes are hard to get because of the cutbacks. Fortunately for me, I have priority registration because I am part of my school's disability center. That being said, college is still like anything else in the adult world, sometimes it's the last place you want to be.

Even at times during that same successful spring semester of my freshman year I felt that community college just wasn't working out. I became increasingly frustrated with the lack of support. I would get very nostalgic about wanting to go back to the high school and see my old comfort people like my aide Kathy. It really seemed tempting to just drop out. But, then I realize that this is just another phase of getting used to a new place. Every transition I went through from elementary school had the same kind of 'I just want to bail' phase. So, I just had to remind myself that it was temporary. I also knew I was a strong and resilient student. So, I decided to stay.

After so many tumultuous experiences during this stage of education my advice to parents and individuals on the spectrum is to be patient. Transition is a gradual process and it doesn't happen overnight. Also, insure a support network that will help you or your loved one navigate through their changing times.

Chapter 17

"You don't know what it's like to live in my body!"

"I would have never known you are autistic had you not told me!" is a comment I often hear when people learn I have autism. Unlike other disabilities autism has no discernible physical features. Therefore, while I may come across to many as "normal" some people come to the erroneous conclusion that my life is that of a typical female college student. One that succeeds at a mainstream college with little or no help. But what people don't understand is that my life is not as straight forward as it may seem. I still face my share of challenges. My disability sees to it. The only people who truly understand my challenges are my parents who have to deal with me 24/7, and my support people who I see regularly. I sometimes feel that I am a disabled person stuck in a body of a typical person. Another disadvantage I have is that my autism is not as impairing compared to those who are nonverbal or have limited speech. Because I am generally aware of my surroundings, most social cues and express myself using appropriate language, I become more of an enigma to people trying to understand my disability. At the same time, it's very tough to perform on the same level as someone without a disability because, as I've explained I have to keep a reign on my socially unacceptable stimming tendencies. Before leaving my house part of my morning routine is doing a quick mental assessment so as to insure that my urges are all in tact.

One of the biggest frustrations and challenges I have is trying to achieve age appropriate goals. For example, I hate it when people get on my case about learning how to drive. It's not that I think I'm incapable of driving but it's the fear and anxiety associated with driving that holds me back. Also, I'm concerned as to whether or not I can stay unrelentingly alert for long stretches. I guess I can drive around with a sign on the back of my car stating "Caution. Autistic Driver Behind the Wheel" but I'm not sure I'll get any sympathy from L.A. drivers. Another issue I have in achieving age appropriate goals is mild motor problems. Most of the time I have relatively good motor skills and it doesn't get in the way of achieving most self-care tasks. However, there are tasks that I have a hard time completing on my own. For instance, I can't pull my hair back in the traditional ponytail, put on my own makeup, trim my own nails or cook meals without supervision. I understand that I can get better at these skills with practice but I find it easier and convenient to have someone help me along. We all have our limitations, whether we are neuro-typical or autistic, parents need to keep expectations realistic.

Being independent is a mixed bag. In fact I think it's overrated. I have discussed this numerous times throughout my book but here my intention is to clearly explain why I find the concept nerve wracking. If you took a poll and asked parents of all other individuals on the spectrum if they dreamed of living independent lives, their response would echo a resounding "Yes". While being independent is ideal and crucial if you want to be a functioning member in society, it has its drawbacks. For instance one of my friends is nonverbal and she has an aide who accompanies her to school and public places etc. Although my friend would want my life any day, at least she has someone there all the time who can give her guidance and can give her backup when things go south.

With me, I don't have that luxury of having a safe person with me all the time like she does so I have to rely on my strategies and tools to get through the day independently. Some days it's easy to navigate with no support but other days especially when there is a lot on my plate getting through the day isn't easy. I know not everyone will agree with me but I want to give you my perspective on this issue. With independence comes responsibility and sometimes it becomes a bit much. I need to find a balance.

Believe it or not there are times where I would rather be autistic than be "typical." The pressure to conform to the same expectations as my typical peers is greater on me because I am not as affected with my disability as are others. This causes me to feel "on the fence" when it comes to my identity. I can get by without being a curiosity to people but at the same time I don't feel "typical" either. This causes me to scramble between the neurotypical world and the world of autism.

Although I have come a long way in learning strategies to manage my stress, there are still times when self-management just fails me. For instance when the triggers are mounting and I have no outlet to deregulate I sometimes randomly shout out a loud "MEAT". The reason why I chose the word meat as my tension releasing strategy is because I picture myself literally pounding a piece a meat when I'm feeling frustrated.

This visualization technique actually keeps me from pounding on something or someone else. Of course, I can't find a piece a meat to pound every time I get worked up so I have to rely on saying the actual word verbally.

Even though I understand that as I get older and get more practice in basic living skills things will become easier but I'm realistic enough to know that life will always be a challenge. It has and will continue to be a long and arduous journey. That I know is the basis of the human condition. Regardless if someone with autism is considered severely impacted or mildly impacted, we all face various and often mysterious individual challenges by simply living in a society run by those not afflicted. Therefore the point of this next chapter is to share what area of this disorder I do know.

Chapter 18

The Ranch: where I found my group

During the summer of 2011 my behaviorist Heather introduced me to a ranch that she helps out during the weekends. The ranch was designed to help children and teens with various disabilities. Heather thought it was a good idea to give it a try since it would be a good opportunity to expand my social circle. I went to the summer camp that was offered by the ranch where I would learn to become a volunteer and run the ranch as well as having fun and being with the animals. One of my friends was also attending the camp so at least there will be one person there that I know and feel comfortable with. At the beginning, I felt a little anxious since the experience was new to me but after a little pep talk with Heather I was able to adjust well and start opening up.

A typical day begins with doing ranch chores then we would do "round-up" in which everyone would gather in a circle and do a game in which each person in the group would share something about themselves. Next, we would separate into two groups to do different activities such as taking care of the horses, arts and crafts and a daily cooking activity. The two groups would rotate so each group has a chance to do all the activities.

My favorite part of the camp day was learning how to take care of animals. Even though I went horseback riding numerous times before attending camp, I learned a lot about tacking, grooming, feeding, leading as well as other aspects of horse care. I also learned how to take care of the other animals such as bunny rabbits, guinea pigs and chickens. Overall, I had a really positive experience that led me to find out how to volunteer during the year.

During the 2011-2012 school year, I decided to attend the "Rancher's Club" where we meet once a month and do a lot of the same activities like we did during summer camp. I got closer with the other teens that I had bonded with. Somehow, the teens who attended the ranch were different from the teens with whom I attended high school. They seem very secure with themselves and are more accepting of other's differences. I'm usually very quiet around new people but I felt more open and talkative to the people at the ranch. In fact, when playing the game two truths and a lie everyone thought I was a very social person when in fact it was a lie since I'm normally very shy and timid. After years of searching for a group and being unsuccessful, I finally found a group of people that I identified with.

The ranch was also a resource where I met someone who I now consider one of my closest friends.

The woman who started the ranch has a daughter who has epilepsy but is seizure free. Because of the positive impact horses had on her daughter is why she opened the ranch in the first place. Heather thought that the daughter would be a good match for me and thought I should pursue her as a friend. As usual, I was a little nervous of approaching her and asking to hang out but with the assistance of Heather I was able to muster up the courage. Luckily she agreed. On our first outing we decided to hang out at the ranch since we were both familiar with that setting. As it turns out, we had a lot in common. Like me, she has a good sense of humor and we both had to overcome a lot of hardships. Unlike some of my other friendships in the past, she was very punctual and always followed through when we planned outings. Although we suffer from different conditions and she is almost five years younger than I am, I consider her to be one of my greatest friends and I'm very thankful to Heather for introducing us.

Chapter 19

Putting my voice out there

During my second year of college, I decided that I wanted to put myself out there by presenting at conferences. Writing an autobiography was the driving force. I was fed up with the fact that there was not enough self advocates with autism (especially adults) and how some neurotypical experts kept making stereotypes and generalizations about autism spectrum disorders. I figured if I want to see a change in how autism is perceived by the general public, I would have to be the one to advocate and tell the world what people like me need and what would help us live successful and fulfilling lives.

The first presentation I did that year was for a parent meeting at my old school district that my former behaviorist Rachel was hosting. Two years before, I did a similar presentation for the parents but it was different in the sense that I could talk about my experience in college as well as sharing excerpt from my book. In fact, one mom cried when she heard me speak because her son asked her about why he was different from the rest of the kids. My dad videotaped the whole speech. Even though I was afraid of watching it myself because I thought my voice sounded bad and low, I got a lot of compliments which gave me more confidence in public speaking. Another opportunity I have in putting myself out there is with the FRED Conference. (A national coalition of special needs professionals and families addressing housing issues.)

My mom's friend who has a teenage son with autism was putting a conference together addressing the issue of housing for adults with disabilities. There aren't a lot of options out there for this demographic so it was the perfect opportunity to learn about some ideas and solutions to address this ever growing population. My part in the conference was to be a co-moderator for a panel of experts and parents who run different programs. My job was to ask questions to a variety of panelists. It was a little nerve wracking at first since I was on a stage in front of 200 people and I was holding a microphone. Being voice conscious, I was afraid that I would sound horrible and everyone would notice. I had to remind myself that everyone there would like to hear what I had to say so I felt really confident. One panelist in particular really stuck with me. He was talking about how most programs focus too much on independence and should instead focus on the concept of interdependence. When I heard this speaker talk about interdependence, I started to reflect on my own life. For my entire school career the goal was for me to be independent. It was engraved in my IEPs and it was expected from my parents and my support people. Interdependence seems like a healthy balance between being both independent and dependent at once.

I was glad that a professional realizes the amount of anxiety that people like me have about becoming independent instead of joining the tribe of numerous autism experts stressing "independence" as the ultimate goal. I was also able to talk a little bit about my experience of growing up on the spectrum and why it's important to be careful of not trying to make individuals like myself feel bad about being who they are.

Being a part of the FRED Conference has helped me gain recognition for people with special needs as well as an opportunity to support a movement that pushes for the advancement of adult services.

Chapter 20

My "Big Sister" Mentor

During the end of my second year of college I began to crave a mentor in my life. A mentor that was neither a therapist nor psychologist. In high school my aide fulfilled that role. But now, as a college junior, my craving had turned into longing. My mom noticed that I was staying home a lot and got somewhat concerned. Since she is so heavily involved in the autistic community she just picked up the phone. We were then referred to an agency in the San Fernando Valley.

I was nervous meeting with the coordinator since I didn't know what I wanted to tell her and I didn't want my mom do all the talking. With the help of Heather, I was able to break it down and come up with a criteria. It consisted of the following: I wanted someone who was at least a few years older. I was looking for a mentor not a friend. Plus, it would feel awkward having someone my age hold some authority over me. I wanted someone who drives, has similar interests and is, of course, dependable. I met with the lady and explained to her who I was looking for. Luckily, she was able to find someone right away thanks to mom and her connections. When the coordinator told me all about my new mentor, I immediately, sight unseen, fell in love with her. Her name was Amanda and she is a young woman in her late 20's who loves fashion and watching movies. The only downside was that I had to wait a whole week to meet her. When I finally met Amanda in person, I was shocked by what I saw. She was wearing mostly black, wore spiky jewelry, had stretched ears and a curvy figure. Seeing her appearance, I jumped to the conclusion that we weren't a good match.

However, she had a very bubbly personality and was genuinely excited to begin working with me so I decided to give her a chance. For our first outing, we decided to go to Venice Beach. I would see Amanda every week usually on a Friday which was my day off from school. Although Amanda presented herself well when I interviewed her, I still felt nervous going out in the community with her alone. One reason was because I didn't know her very well and I was worried that she wouldn't not want to do the activities or go to the stores I enjoy since we had such different taste. Over the course of the first outing, I began to warm up to her. She has a very funny sense of humor and was making me laugh. For instance, we were trying on different sunglasses at the Venice beach boardwalk and Amanda put on these pink sunglasses and did a silly impression. I laughed. I was beginning to find her quite entertaining. Even though Amanda lived an alternative lifestyle we both shared the same desire to be playful. After our first outing, I realized that Amanda was the best match even though it took my mom awhile to get use to her tattoos. But Amanda did not act like she looked. She is very nurturing and responsible. Even though on most of our outings we have fun like friends would, there were times Amanda would have to give me constructive feedback on my behavior. These were times when I would, for instance, start acting impulsively and looking at things inside her car or blurting out random words. Regardless, I felt happy to have her in my life and I consider her to be my "big sister". I feel I can turn to her whenever I am having a bad day and can tell her anything. I always look forward to our weekly outings.

Unfortunately after three months of working together, the agency decided to lay off Amanda unexpectedly. I found this out a day before I was supposed to meet with her. Both my mom and I were shocked. There had been no indication. I felt devastated like I was torn into little pieces because I really liked Amanda and we were really getting to know each other. When we met with the coordinator, she told us that the reason why Amanda was let go was because she didn't have the right credentials. They changed their qualifications standards in which all the staff working for the agency must have a degree in working with adults with disabilities or special education. In Amanda's case, she had a teaching credential for elementary school children so under the new requirements she would not be able to qualify to work with my demographic. After hearing this rationale, I was angry at the agency for having such warped priorities. We were a good fit! In addition, the coordinator went on to tell me that I should be more focused on learning independent living skills than having a mentor for recreational purposes. Wow. That took nerve. I just don't understand how an agency who claims they employ "person centered" programming can turn their back on their clients by telling them what their priorities should be. After that meeting, my mom and I decided that we should probably part ways with the agency since they seemed to care more about money than me.

Now comes the quandary of finding a brand new mentor. So, Heather and I started brainstorming again. She's great for that. We decided that using my support network might save steps. The only problem with finding a new person is that it is a long process and you have to go through so many people until you find the right one. Although my experience with Amanda did prove otherwise.

Since it was August and school was going to start in a couple of weeks, I knew I wasn't going to find someone permanently in that short amount of time. Then my mom came up with the idea of contacting Amanda and suggesting that she work with us directly. At first, I thought Amanda wouldn't take our offer. I thought she might have considered it unprofessional. But, what do you know? I was wrong. She was in and I was giddy. Just like a fairy tale, this story had a happy ending. Ever since leaving high school, I never felt that anyone would replace my aide and mentor Kathy since she was so exceptional. But she did with an added bonus. We were closer in age than Kathy and I. That meant we could actually go out and *do* things together. Lucky me.

Chapter 21

My Current Life

As I wrap up this book, I'd like to give you a glimpse of the last year. I am closing up my third year of college and about to transfer to a four year University. It's been a long road in getting to where I am now. In this chapter I am going to talk about how autism affects me currently, my anxiety about transitioning to college and what is needed to circumnavigating both.

Being that I plan to live in a dorm this coming year I'm in need of finding someone who can teach me independent living skills. My mom and I decided to talk to our regional center case manager about finding someone who can come to our house as well as my dorm room. It took awhile to get the whole process underway being that we needed to get the funding, of course, before anything else. It wasn't until November when we got into contact with a supported living agency who was going to provide us with someone to match my needs. The woman who ran the agency wanted to meet with me to learn what specific skills I needed to work on. I told her that I recently had a bad experience with another agency and was therefore, this time, approaching it all with caution. This woman seemed really interested in what I had to say so I decided to go with her agency. A few weeks later one of their representatives contacted me so as to schedule an introductory meeting. Apparently she wasn't just representing the agency, she was instead the very person who would be working with me. This miscommunication was the first indication that this agency was not what it seemed to be. For one thing, they didn't consult with me in selecting this person which should have been a given.

Be that as it may, I shunned my first instinct and decided to give her a chance because she seemed nice enough to deal with. However, over the course of our working together, I began to get the feeling that it just wasn't working out. Even though this person was really good in helping me in the kitchen, she seemed to lack good judgment when it came to car safety. For instance, when she picked me up for our first weekend together there was another person in the car to observe our session since she was new to the agency. She hadn't even told me. So, as a result of this 'observer', I had to sit in the back seat with a broken seatbelt and she didn't even seem to notice. I felt unsafe when riding with her since I was under her care and I was worried about liability issues since I don't know how safe a driver she is. When I approached her about this, she didn't seem to think it was abig deal and had a calm almost condescending attitude towards me. At that moment I felt that her heart wasn't into her job. She was way too passive. In addition she really didn't take initiative in our sessions and I just felt we weren't going anywhere . . . and definitely not in her car! If anything, I felt this was a waste of my precious time since I had a lot of schoolwork and other activities planned for the weekends. Bottom line is I knew we weren't going to work so I decided to stop the service altogether. My story in dealing with adult services shows that we still have a long way to go in terms of developing effective adult programming. In most state funded services, the quality is not there since the selected staff are not appropriately trained in dealing with adults with disabilities. This is very unfortunate since most people rely on regional center funding to get what they vitally need.

That being the end result I still have a lot of anticipatory anxiety about moving into the dorm because I don't feel my living skill set is where I planned on it being prior to this huge transition. Regardless, I have a loving support system that will believe in and stand by me during these hard times as so many times they have before.

But, even with this belief in place, in anticipation of this daunting upcoming independence, I found myself wanting to re-visit interests I had when I was younger. I suddenly found myself wanting to collect Hello Kitty and Disney Princess items again as well as watching old Spongebob episodes. I know I mentioned about being an avid fan of these cartoons during my middle school years and how they pervaded my everyday life but this time is was different. I know that there is a time and place to engage in these interests whereas before I didn't understand this concept. At first I felt that I was regressing when I found myself drawn to these preadolescent icons. However after talking to Heather, I realized that I was just exploring old interests and that there are adults out there that don't have autism who watch cartoons and collect all kinds of crazy kid things. That perspective helped me to me lose some of the self-judgment I tend to entertain during tricky times. So, even though I've made so much progress to the point that people wouldn't know that I have autism, I would not consider myself to be recovered from it nor if I ever will be. I still feel challenged in group situations and have sensory issues. As for repetitive behavior, I still do it. To this day I'm still trying to get a handle on my spinning thoughts and have more confidence in my abilities. It's a process but I'm getting there. Somehow I am still able to get through the day without any of these deficiencies interfering with my life.

I am currently in the process of searching for a four year university. I went on a bunch of college tours to see which colleges I wanted to apply. I looked at three colleges but one that I particularly have my eye on was a private college that has a view that overlooks Los Angeles. What I liked about it was that it was close to home and it was a small campus. To my luck, I applied and got accepted to my first choice for college. When I got my acceptance letter I felt very accomplished since I worked so hard to get good grades at the community college. In addition, I also found out that I also qualified to get an A.A. degree and will be walking in my school's graduation ceremony in June 2013. While it was exciting that I got accepted into a four year university, it is also nerve wracking at the same time. I will be living in a dorm for the first time and I am feeling anxious about moving away from home for the first time since for the last 21 years of my life I have been living at home with my parents. I am also unsure if I will be able to make new friends once I am at my new school. The good news is that my school is 20-30 minutes away from home and so I can go home on the weekends and I can still keep my same support people like my behaviorist/ life coach Heather and my new mentor Jessica.

Chapter 22

Conclusion

I want to thank you for reading my book. My goal was for readers to thoroughly understand the complexities that go hand and hand with living on the spectrum. I'm hoping that I have reached this aim. As I said in the beginning, I wanted to write this book to give families of younger children hope. I also wanted to educate neurotypicals, especially professionals, on what would be the best way to help individuals with autism.

I also want to remind you that every person with autism is different. My experience maybe different from you or your child. This is not a story about someone who recovers from autism, since I truly believe you never fully recover from the symptoms. One is only able to mask them.

Although most of my book covers my childhood and adolescence, I do talk a little bit about my experience as a college student and how navigating the world of adulthood is like navigating a mine field. The fact that I.E.P.s are not carried over from high school is tragic. Sadly 40% of students wanting to pursue higher education without the necessary accommodations drop out. I've been able to deal with the limited resources because I got creative but moreover I was/am fortunate enough to have established a support network of people who are going to help me get through.

As I said, the biggest reason why I wrote this memoir was to educate the masses. Even though the first inkling about autism was spawned by Martin Luther circa 1797 today it is still a mystery to most. By nature humans are social beings so when they encounter someone like me where social situations overwhelm them, they often don't know what to do.

Oftentimes, the natural reaction of the neurotypical public is to try to "fix" and "normalize" us. While this may sound desirable for some families, for me this "normalization" moment is more harmful than helpful.

As you read through my memoir trying to "fit in" has caused me to feel conflicted and in need of masking my true identity.

As much as my aim is to educate I have also been the student. I have learned a lot from having autism. When you have any disability your life is altered in some ways. What I have learned from having autism is that it taught me that it is ok to ask for help from people. Some individuals on the autism spectrum (believe me I have met them) are ashamed about their diagnosis and are afraid to open up. I understand how they feel since the majority of the population just don't get it. Autism has taught me to accept myself for who I am and that being other than the 'norm' is ok. I used to be so down on myself for being different from everyone else but then I realized I have my own developmental path and I go at my own rate. The last thing I want to tell parents and professionals is to embrace your son or daughter. There are some days where it's challenging especially if your child has some behavioral problems. But in the end, your child is a person and deserves love and attention just like any other child. Also, take your child out in the community and do fun activities together. The more experience your child has going out in the community the more social skills he or she will attain. My parents would often take me out in the community. We also did a lot of traveling. As a result of these varied experiences as well as all the expertise and kindness I received from my support team, I am not only able to grow as a person, but grow into what I consider now to be a viable, unique and important member of society

CPSIA information can be obtained at www.ICGtesting.com
Printed in the USA
LVOW11s1157061214

417441LV00001B/49/P